I0605360

The
Soul Instinct

The Soul Instinct

Beatrice Dixon

G

Gallery Books

New York Amsterdam/Antwerp London
Toronto Sydney/Melbourne New Delhi

Gallery Books
An Imprint of Simon & Schuster, LLC
1230 Avenue of the Americas
New York, NY 10020

First Gallery Books hardcover edition January 2026

GALLERY BOOKS and colophon are registered trademarks of Simon & Schuster, LLC

Interior design by Alexis Minieri

Manufactured in the United States of America

1 3 5 7 9 10 8 6 4 2

Library of Congress Control Number: 2025942327

ISBN 978-1-6680-4973-0
ISBN 978-1-6680-4975-4 (ebook)

To my grandmothers Margaret Booker Mills Turner and Margaret Strother; my mother, Stephanie Turner; and my ancestors and guides.

Contents

Foreword

Beatrice Dixon is my best female-founder friend, a little sister of sorts, and one of the rare people in my life who brings both comfort and spirit at the same time. Our connection is one of those miraculous, divinely orchestrated friendships that instantly felt like home.

We met in the earliest, most uncertain days of Covid-19, on a group call with other beauty and wellness founders who had come together in solidarity—to share ideas, to help one another weather the storm, to remind ourselves we weren't alone. I said something on that call, and at the end Bea said in her gentle voice: "I'd love to talk to the lady from goop." That small moment led to a side conversation, and that side conversation turned into one of the most important relationships in my life.

Since then, Bea and I have been walking this founder's road

side by side. We laugh, we weep, we adventure, we have FaceTime calls at all hours where we troubleshoot or commiserate, we do wellness practices together, and we call each other back to center when the weight of leading companies threatens to break us. Our friendship has become a kind of medicine. I truly believe that when we're together, our nervous systems find equilibrium. We heal each other. We remind each other that yes, the path is hard—but also beautiful, sacred, and worth every ounce of energy we put into it.

What Bea has written in these pages is a gift. Her story is an anthem of resilience, intuition, and the radical power of believing in yourself even when the world underestimates you. She has lived a life that could have broken her, and instead she has alchemized every hardship into strength, wisdom, and love—for herself, for her customers, for her community.

Reading this book is like sitting across from Bea with a cup of tea, feeling her honesty, her vulnerability, and her strength radiating through every word. She has the rare ability to let you in so fully that you come away not just knowing her story but also knowing yourself a little better.

It is my honor to call her my sister, my friend, and one of the most inspiring founders I know. I cannot wait for you to meet her here.

—Gwyneth Paltrow

Introduction

"What are you lying about?" my mother asked me. It was 2018, and we were sitting in my car after a doctor's appointment—me behind the wheel, my mom next to me. While I'd mostly gotten a clean bill of health, the doctor mentioned that I had elevated thyroid levels. Nothing especially out of the ordinary, certainly nothing dangerous, but I knew my mom was going to have questions. She'd come along just to keep me company, but now I'd have to pay for that. The doctor's office was about forty minutes from my apartment in Atlanta, so I knew we were about to get into it.

"What are you talking about?" I responded.

"Beatrice. We don't have thyroid problems in our family," she said. "For you to develop one out of nowhere, you are lying to yourself about something."

There's an old wives' tale that says thyroid problems are a

result of not living your truth. If you're avoiding facing your problems, or denying them altogether, your body will turn against you, or so the story goes. My mother, being the Black mother she is, holds tight to these tales.

"I'm not lying about anything," I said.

She looked at me like only a mother can look at a daughter. She didn't open her mouth, but her face said it all. *Who are you kidding?* And *What's going on?* And *It's time to come clean.*

That look broke something open inside of me. I burst into tears. Sobbing. Snot running down my face. Gasping for breath. All of it. I had been holding so much in, scared to voice out loud the fears and doubts that had been plaguing me, and now here they were, spilling out my eyeballs and running out my nose.

"I need you to calm down," my mom said. "You're driving."

I pulled over at the first opportunity, wiping my tears and trying to collect myself. My mother has always been my safety net. She doesn't solve my problems for me—in fact, she usually doesn't even chime in. She lets me make mistakes, because she knows the importance of figuring stuff out for myself. But if my life has been a tightrope walk, she really has been the net. I have to get across on my own, but if I go down, she's there to break my fall. To remind me it will all be OK.

In the passenger seat, my mother shifted her body so she was looking directly at me. "I've never said this to you, Bea, but I'm going to right now, because you need to hear it," she said. "Any day you live doing *anything* you don't want to do, it's time wasted. Do you know why? Because you're going to die.

We could drive home right now and get hit by a truck. Would you be OK to die right now? On your deathbed, would you be OK with the decisions that you have made?"

"No," I said between sobs.

"Well then you need to get your shit together," she said. "Because you *are* going to die. Hopefully not until you're old, but you could for damn sure die when you're young. So if you aren't being honest with yourself, if you're living a life that doesn't serve you, then you need to deal with that *now*. Because every moment you are living a lie, that is a life-or-death moment."

My mother had never leveled with me like this. We were always honest with each other, but like I said, she rarely offered unsolicited advice. She didn't intervene; instead she waited for me to ask. Now here she was, basically saying, *Bitch, wake up! What the fuck are you doing?*

If every existence can be divided into a before and after, that singular moment in the car was my turning point. Not when I moved to Atlanta, or when I started my own business, or when I left my husband, or when I made my first million. Each of those were important events—moments and decisions that have influenced the course of my life. But this exchange with my mom, it was a soul shift. It *saved* my life. I'd never considered my mortality before. I was so busy getting through one day and then the next that I never thought about dying. But I also didn't think about *living*. I was just trying to get by—working myself to the bone, suffering in an unhappy relationship, and feeling exhausted in my body and my spirit. I was lonely and overworked and burned out. I had been living in darkness, but that day my mother lit a candle. Nobody had ever been so real with me. It was a wake-up call of the highest order—a reminder that you can *choose* how you live your life. In the chaos of my day-to-day, I had forgotten that simple truth.

This short conversation with my mother changed how I live, and how I see the world. It started me on the path of doing the deep internal work that was necessary to heal from my past and allowed me to make space for my future. I had forgotten who I was, and who I'd always been, and this was the first step toward finding that person again.

It was the lesson of my lifetime.

*

Since that day in the car, which was about seven years ago now, I have been on a healing journey. That doesn't mean that everything was bad before or everything is good now. Life is complicated, and that's what makes it beautiful. It doesn't even mean that I stepped out of the car that day and changed my life on a dime. But that conversation gave me a new perspective and started me on a path to make some big decisions. It helped me hone my soul instinct, because I finally started spending time with myself, and pausing to really listen to my inner voice. I had a new lens through which to look at every opportunity and decide what deserves my energy and what should be let go. Not that letting go is easy. It's one of the hardest acts in the world, in fact. But easy has never been what drives me.

Today, most of my energy goes toward my business. I launched The Honey Pot Company, the world's first plant-derived feminine care brand, in 2014. I'll get more into the details of creating that company later, but the short version is this: I was suffering with bacterial vaginosis for almost a year. If you've never had it—well, you're lucky. It's smelly and uncomfortable and altogether unpleasant. I tried everything—over-the-counter creams, prescription meds, whatever absurd method Google suggested would provide relief—and nothing worked. Then, one night, my long-deceased grandmother visited me in a dream and gave me the ingredients I'd need to cure to my BV once and for all. I woke up, immediately jotted down the ingredients on a notepad, and used my background in pharmaceutical work to formulate a concoction that cured me nearly overnight. (It took about four days, but when you've been battling with a smelly, uncomfortable vagina for a year, that's fast enough.)

> It's a company with a soul and a mission: to empower and heal humans with vaginas.

In the ten years since, together with a team of partners and supporters and colleagues, I've built the company from a handful of people making washes in my kitchen to a multimillion-dollar business with seventy-five employees and products in Target, CVS, Walgreens, Walmart, and more. We started with washes, but now we make wipes, lubes, period products, suppositories, and supplements—all of which we sell to more than four million customers worldwide. It's a company with a soul and a mission: to empower and heal humans with vaginas.

Honey Pot is a brand that's anchored in self-care. For me, those values start at home. Building a company requires a lot from a person. It gives so much—emotional and professional fulfillment, financial stability, a platform to speak on important issues and actually be heard—but it takes in return. As the face of Honey Pot, a lot of my life has become public. It can be taxing physically, emotionally, and spiritually . . . especially because I am an introvert. And an empath. And an intuitive. I am someone who lives openly and honestly—the Bea you meet at a party is the same Bea you'll meet in a boardroom. She talks the same and laughs the same and tells the same stories. I don't know how to be any other way. I'm grateful for that, and I think it has served me well, but it also makes me feel quite vulnerable. I'm out there for the world to see. There's no armor. No hiding. My soul is always on display.

> The hard moments are as important as the celebratory ones. Because whatever the circumstance, this moment is all we have.

To keep my business healthy, I need to keep my spirit healthy. I spend a lot of effort on what I call my soul work. That means different things on different days. Meditating. Yoga and Reiki. Connecting with my ancestors. Drinking water. Talking to my intuitive. Of course, I fall off the wagon sometimes—giving myself to my company or to other people at the expense of taking care of myself—because I'm a human being. And not just a human being, but a woman of color trying to grow a business in a world that doesn't necessarily encourage or support that path. But I keep at it and put in the self-work because the one thing I know for damn sure, because my mother made it crystal clear, is that Bea Dixon only has one life. And it is a gift from God to be able to be present in that life, to be in the moment and be OK with it, whatever it is. Maybe somebody just had a baby, maybe someone just died. The hard moments are as important as the celebratory ones. Because whatever the circumstance, this moment is all we have. What my mother wanted to get through to me that day is that any time I am living in denial, it's as if I'm dead already.

Writing this book has been an extension of my soul work. It has offered me the opportunity to reflect on my life and make sense of my past, to celebrate it and heal from it, and to understand how each piece has contributed to the way in which I exist in the world today. It is my story—one with plenty of untraditional twists and turns. Honey Pot is what I'm known for now, but there was so much that came before, because my path to business owner and CEO was not linear.

Still, it was the only journey I could have taken to get to this moment. Everything that came before had to happen for me to be writing this book today. I know that now. Would I do it all the same way again? I'm not sure. Are there moments in my history that I wish hadn't happened? Of course. But all things in order. The past is gone. There is only now. Writing this book has been a rigorous excavation—it has cleared out layers of residue so that I can stand more firmly in the present. It's been hard and empowering and trying and necessary and demanding and a privilege. Just like life.

Honey Pot started from a place of authenticity. I didn't begin the journey by saying "I want to build a company." I just wanted to fix my coochie! I was desperate to heal myself, and helping myself led to helping other people. This book is the same. It is a literal self-help book . . . writing it has helped *my self.* It's the realization of the work I have done and am doing to be the best version of Beatrice Nikka Dixon. I don't presume to know how anyone else lives, or to suggest how anyone else *should* live. In these pages, I only speak for myself. About what was right for me, or how I want to move through the universe. I know from the evolution of Honey Pot that sometimes when you do the work to heal yourself, you can contribute to the healing of others. So this book is for me, but maybe it's for you too. If the work I've done can help you make sense of your life, or see your experiences in a new way, or inspire you to face the present moment with the urgency it deserves, I'm grateful for that. Because at the end of day, your life is your choice. You can choose to live in fear and doubt and in circumstances that aren't serving you—just as I was when I sat down in the literal and figurative driver's seat opposite my mom—or you can choose to take ownership. Me, I chose that day to wake up.

It wasn't easy.

It's ongoing.

I choose it every day.

Chapter One

Origin Story

I was seven or eight years old when my mom started telling me the story of how I arrived on this planet—an epic tale she shares each year on my birthday.

"You were meant to be here," she begins. "It was touch and go for you, but you were a fighter from the beginning . . ."

When you're young and your mom wants to recount the story of your birth, it's a big eye roll. After hearing it the first time, my response for years was basically "Yeah, yeah, I know, I know. You've already told me this." But she shares the tale each year because my entry into this world was a gnarly one.

My mom got pregnant with me when she was twenty-five years old. She wasn't dating my dad, but he had been her first love when she was young. They'd grown apart over the years, but in the spring of 1982, she went to see him, and unbeknownst to her, that visit created a memento. One she hadn't specifically asked for and certainly didn't expect.

My mother had been pregnant twice before—with my older brother, Skip, and, before him, with twins who were born with blue baby syndrome and passed away when they were only a few days old. Since Skip's birth, she had tried unsuccessfully to get pregnant—she tried for long enough that she asked a doctor about it, who basically told her it might never happen again. My mother had a tough upbringing, and her young adulthood wasn't all that easy either. She'd lost two babies, her father and stepmother lived with her, and she was under huge amounts of stress trying to support everyone and make ends meet. That kind of hardship can take a toll, and the doctor made it clear that another pregnancy might not be in her future.

At the time of her visit with my father, my mom was working three jobs in Arlington, Virginia, where she lived. During the day, she worked at a hospice care facility, at night she cleaned schools, and on her days off from those jobs she worked as an in-home hospice worker, helping people whose relatives were passing. It was difficult work—hard on her body and on her spirit—and she was always on her feet, so even though, in the aftermath of her visit with my dad, she was tired and had stomach pains and would get sick from time to time, she chalked all that up to the fact that she was working around the clock. At one point she was feeling some flutters in her abdomen, and her stepmother—my grandmother—suggested she might be pregnant, but her pregnancy test came back negative. That wasn't much of a surprise, since by that point she thought there was basically no way.

In the months after their springtime reunion, my mother and father went their separate ways. They were no longer in each other's lives, and my mom began dating somebody new, a man who was quite wealthy and quite generous with her. As a gift, he bought her a brand-new red convertible. She loved that car! But three days after she picked it up, she was sitting at a traffic light on Virginia Route 7, a two-way, four-lane highway, when the brakes went out of a garbage truck coming down the hill and caused a three-car pile-up. My mom was the third car, and even though the garbage truck was blowing its horn and she could see it coming, she couldn't get out of the way because there was oncoming traffic. The truck tried to downshift to a lower gear to slow down, and it helped, but the momentum of the hill meant it was still moving at a decent clip when it hit that first car, which hit a second car, which hit my mom. Luckily, a police officer was sitting on the other side of the stoplight and saw what happened. He called for help immediately—if he hadn't been there, who knows if emergency workers would have come quickly enough, or if my mom would have even survived. As it was, she broke a knee, hurt her back, and badly bruised her ribs because they jammed into the steering wheel upon impact. Not to mention the fact that her brand-new car was completely totaled. She stayed in the hospital for three days but still didn't know she was pregnant, and no one there realized it either.

After the accident, my mom went back to work. Back then, doctors used compression wraps for injured ribs, so she was cleaning schools and working in hospice care while dealing with her own pain and attempts at healing. That woman is a warrior. Always has been. But she was still feeling the same flutters she'd noticed even before the accident, so at one of her follow-up visits, she mentioned them to her doctor. Now the flutters were in her ribs, and at times they were pretty painful. The doctors did a blood test, which once again showed she wasn't pregnant. He told her the pain was probably due to swelling and trauma from the accident.

Fast-forward a couple of weeks. My mother was at her night job, cleaning the school, and she had a "flutter" that was not just uncomfortable, it was excruciating. Her cousin worked at the school with her and insisted she go straight to the hospital.

When my mom got to the ER, she told the doctor everything—about the accident, her rib pain, the flutters she'd been feeling. "Something is going on," she said to the doctor. "I don't know what it is, but something is not right." The doctor asked her if she was pregnant. "How could I be?" she asked. Not only had she been told that she was unlikely to get pregnant, she had taken two negative pregnancy tests, and she'd been in a pretty horrific car accident—one that would make it nearly impossible for a baby to survive—and now she was walking around with her ribs held tight in a compression wrap.

They did a blood test anyway. "Ma'am, I don't know what that other doctor told you, or where they went wrong, but you're pregnant," the doctor said. "There's no question about it."

My mom had a flood of emotions—shock, because she'd been told over and over again that she wasn't pregnant; fear, because she'd been in a car accident and had her ribs wrapped tight and she didn't know what harm that might have caused her baby; excitement, because she had wanted to get pregnant again, and now she was.

Given all the physical trauma she'd been through recently, the doctor sent my mother in to get a sonogram. But when the sonogram tech rubbed her wand over my mom's pelvis, she saw nothing. No heartbeat. No little bean-shaped fetus. Nothing.

Something wasn't making sense.

"Indulge me," the doctor said to the sonogram technician. "Check under her right rib, where she says the pain is the worst." Sure enough, there I was. It turned out that when the steering wheel jammed into my mom's stomach and ribs, the baby—me—had moved upward, underneath her rib cage.

"I've never seen anything like this," the doctor said. "But I guess there's a first time for everything."

Once it was discovered that my mom was pregnant, the doctors told her they were going to have to perform surgery to move me back down into her pelvis. But before they did that, they were very clear with her that this baby might not survive, and even if it did, there could be a life full of hardship waiting for my mom and her child. My mother's body, and her fetus, had been through a lot of trauma in the last few months. They warned her that I could be born with any number of challenges—brain damage, disfigurement, difficulty breathing, the list went on—and that it was quite likely I wouldn't survive at all. The doctors were not shy about recommending that she terminate her pregnancy.

"If the Good Lord put her wherever he put her, and my baby's still here, then she wants to be here," my mom said. "Everything will be fine."

"How do you know it's a girl?" the doctor asked.

"Trust me," she said. "It's a girl, and if he put her there, she's going to make it." My mother has always had strong faith.

I think everyone's version of "fine" is different, and the doctors had an obligation to warn my mom about the challenges that could lie ahead. They explained that the surgery, which would involve moving my mother's rib to coax me back down, could endanger and perhaps end the pregnancy. They ushered in doctor after doctor to walk her through the risks, each one acting as if she must not have understood what the doctor before them was saying. They brought in social services, and a psychologist. They brought in her father and her stepmom. My mother likes to joke that it was a "how many doctors does it take to screw in a lightbulb?" situation, because they kept telling her and retelling her what could go wrong, but her response never wavered.

"If she's here, she wants to be here."

While my mom never questioned whether she wanted to

keep me and go through with the surgery, she did worry that maybe she should have known she was pregnant or done more to help protect me in her belly. Like so many mothers, she was quick to question herself—*if she had known she was pregnant earlier, could all this hardship have been prevented?*—but the doctors were clear on this too. There was nothing she could have done differently, they said. If anything, it was a miracle that she didn't lose her baby in the accident. The fact that I moved up into her ribs is what saved my life, they said.

Two weeks after my mother learned she was pregnant, she was wheeled in for surgery. It was successful, I survived, and they left me in my mother's womb to let me grow.

My mom carried me for another four months. At this point she was being watched under close care, and over time the doctors could tell I wasn't developing as I should. When my mother was seven months pregnant, they induced labor.

I was born on November 19, 1982, weighing three pounds, nine ounces. I was very premature—born at only seven months—and that underdevelopment combined with the injuries I'd sustained in the womb translated to a whole host of medical issues, to put it mildly. I was born without a nose—just two little holes in my face, the beginnings of nostrils—and a forehead that had not entirely developed, which meant that my brains were essentially exposed. I was sent into surgery immediately. My mother didn't even get to see me before they whisked me away for a twelve-hour operation, one that no one could be sure I'd survive. "Your baby has fingers and toes," they told my mom. "She's alive right now, but we're taking her to surgery." That was all the information she was given.

The first twenty-four to seventy-two hours would be critical, the doctors told my mother, and there were a handful of touch-and-go moments. One night during that window, after my mom had already been sent home, she got a call from the hospital telling her I wasn't going to make it. In fact, they had already called the clergyman to be by my side in my final moments. She lived fifteen miles from the hospital, but my mother hopped in the car and, to hear her tell it, "drove like a maniac," because there was no way her baby was going to be by herself if she was going to die. Of course, my mom got pulled over, but after she told the policeman where she was headed, he told her to follow him. He led her through some traffic and she made it to the hospital in record time.

Our ancestors are our spiritual base, especially in critical moments.

My mom is part Black and part Native American, and her Native side is very strong. The connection to our family ancestry is very deep—our ancestors are our spiritual base, especially in critical moments. "I believe in my ancestors more so than I believe in the person standing in front of me," my mom always says. So, on that drive, she started talking. She communicated mostly with her mother, who passed when my mom was eight years old but has always been one of her guiding spirits. And what my mom heard in response, clear as day, was that I was going to survive. She didn't need to worry, because I would be OK. And not only OK, but great. I was destined for big things, my grandmother said, and this was but a small obstacle on my way to fulfilling that destiny. My mom arrived at the hospital and told the doctors what she knew—that I wasn't going anywhere.

"I don't know who told you that, but it's not what we're seeing," the doctors said.

About four hours later, my health began to improve. "Your faith must be very powerful," the doctors told her. "Normally these babies pass."

"My baby isn't just any 'normal' baby," my mom said. "Her ancestors blessed her. She's got a job to do, and she ain't going nowhere until her ancestors are ready for her." Over time, as my mother knew I would, I got stronger. She and my grandfather and stepgrandmother and aunts and uncles would come to see me, and pray over me, and my mother was confident I would be fine, even if the doctors weren't.

I stayed in the hospital for five months—the first four were in Arlington and then I was medevaced to Children's National Hospital in DC. I was jaundiced, and because I had no nose, I couldn't suck properly. I had to be fed little droplets of formula through what was essentially a baby doll bottle, and because I was so tiny, I was dressed in baby doll clothes. I literally fit into the palm of a hand. But unlike a baby doll, I was not held constantly—I could not get skin-to-skin contact or the usual cuddles because I was in an incubator, hooked up to tubes every which way, helping me breathe and keeping me alive. I underwent three surgeries. Eventually, the doctors used cadaver skin as well as skin from my mother and underneath my own little baby arm to construct a nose and forehead and generally transform my face to one that could breathe and eat on its own.

At some point in my multi-month hospital stay, my mother's boyfriend at the time—the same insanely wealthy one who bought her the red convertible—paid for one of the foremost surgeons in the world to travel from Germany to Washington, DC, to do a final operation to my forehead and help protect my brain. That's why I ended up at Children's National Hospital. My mom's relationship with this man didn't last very long, and I have no memory of him, but I am forever grateful to him nonetheless. He took care of my mother when she needed it most and ensured she didn't get saddled with medical bills. He made sure I had the best of the best when it came to care. He's not in my life or my mother's anymore, but he will always be a part of our story.

There were so many surgeries—in the beginning and, actually, for the first couple years of my life —but they did a good job! To this day it is really difficult and awkward for me to wear sunglasses because my nose doesn't have a bridge, but you wouldn't know it from looking at me. In fact, I didn't even know that anything about my face was "different" until my mother told me years later.

At five months old, I was released from the hospital. I was still tiny. Upon my arrival at home, my grandfather punched a pillow to create a little nest, and I was small enough to fit perfectly in that indent—my mom still has the photo. A bunch of us lived in that house: my mother, my pop-pop Osborne, his wife Margaret, and my older brother, Skip. Later, my mom would get remarried, which would add my brother Frankie to our mix, and my uncle Stevie would move in with us too. But when I got home from the hospital, the five of us were plenty.

My mother was working multiple jobs and hustling to make a living to support her babies. Because my mom worked the way she did, my grandmother Margaret—my mom's stepmother—was my caretaker. (My pop-pop had a thing for Margarets—all of his ladies shared that name! My mother's mother was a Margaret too.) My grandma Margaret was a second mother to me, and I was her precious baby.

She was a white woman who loved her sugar and loved her liquor. She wore dentures, and to this day I remember her taking her teeth out and putting them down on the table—I always got a kick out of that! She was a force of nature who put everything she had into making sure I survived. We were extremely close until the day she died. I couldn't sneeze without her being right there! And, like any good grandma, she fattened me up quickly and transformed me from a frail little thing to a big-boned hearty baby. It was to the point that even the doctors were impressed. At my checkups, they'd look at me and ask my grandma, "How did you get this extra-fat juicy baby? How'd you do that??" They called me a miracle child—the doctors would trot me out to the waiting room and say to other patients, "You want to believe in miracles? This girl right here is a miracle."

When my mom would tell me this story, she never used the word *miracle*—I don't think she wanted it to go to my head—but the notion was there. The world had conspired against the two of us, but we could not be deterred. It was an amazing tale, but when she shared it at my ninth, tenth, eleventh birthday . . . well, I didn't want to hear it. I was a regular kid, not exactly one to appreciate the poignance of my defying-the-odds origin story when I could be out playing with my friends or watching *Reading Rainbow* or *Fraggle Rock*. I'm inclined to say I lost sight of the meaning of what she was telling me, but the truth is that I didn't lose it—I never saw it in the first place. I was too young to appreciate what she'd been through.

Today, as an adult, I have a deep respect for my beginning. I can see how it set the tone for my entire existence. I had to fight to live, even from a young age, and there are some amazing traits that come from that—resilience and strength and independence—but it was also traumatic. For me and also for my mom. She has never said so explicitly, and she has certainly never complained about any of it (and between a car accident and a premature labor and a baby with all sorts of medical challenges, there was plenty to complain about), but I think part of the reason my mom continues to remind me each year of how it all went down is that she wants me to appreciate what a wonder it was for me to make it at all, let alone for me to be a forty-two-year-old successful entrepreneur who is physically healthy and thriving. The fact that I am sitting here today as a happy and full and voluptuous and beautiful and open and connected human?

That is a gift. Now that I'm an adult, I can respect why she needs me to understand, not only because she doesn't want me to lose perspective, but because we were the only two people who were there through it all. She witnessed the beauty but also the terror of my entry into this world, and that can be both a blessing and a burden. I can appreciate her wanting to offload a little bit of that, or at least to share the weight of it. Despite the many miracles my mother witnessed throughout her short pregnancy and my infancy, she must have also had moments that were awful, and a lot of them. When I ask her about it, she shrugs it off. "I didn't have time to be worried about me, I was too busy worrying about you," she'll say. "I can look back at it now and think, how did I do that? But you do it because when it comes time to push, you push."

I had to fight to live, even from a young age, and there are some amazing traits that come from that—resilience and strength and independence—but it was also traumatic.

No matter how tough it got, my mother never gave up on me. She sat next to that incubator, when all the medical professionals were still wondering if I was even going to survive, and she would whisper: "Beatrice Nikka, you are far greater than they believe." I could have come out with one arm and one toe and two heads and she would have been like, "That's my baby, she's going to be fine." There's beauty in a love that fierce, and I'm sure it's from her that I inherited my will to survive.

In fact, there's so much that I inherited from my mother. She has been my greatest teacher. She has also, in many ways, been my greatest protector. Even before I was born, she protected me with all her might, and I feel indebted to her for that. She could have taken the doctor's advice and made a different choice about her pregnancy, and I don't think anyone would have blamed her. Every woman should have the power to choose what she does with her own body, and it is nobody's business but our own what we do with our vaginas and our uteri, and had my mother made a different decision she would have been well within her right. And yet, she did not. She knew the challenges she was accepting when she decided to keep this baby. I'm grateful to her for never giving up on me, even when everyone told her she should.

Still, because of the circumstances around my birth, and because I was so fragile as a baby, for most of my life my mom treated me as precious. And not just in the regular protective-mom way. Because of my nose reconstruction, I wasn't even allowed to fall, because the doctors worried that if I did, my nose could get pushed back into my forehead. It's not that she loved me more than she loved my brothers—that certainly wasn't the case, though if you ask Skip he'll be sure to tell you I got all the attention—but I was delicate, and a lot of focus was on me even once I was out of the hospital. I was also the only girl in the family, and while my brothers got their own education in how to survive as Black men in the world, my mother had different messages for me because she knew my experience would be separate from theirs. She couldn't see the future, but she'd lived for two and a half decades by the time I was born, and she'd been through plenty of her own hard times. She knew what she wanted to prepare me for, and what she wanted to protect me from.

It's tough to know sometimes which parts of my upbringing were a result of my unusual birth story, and what was just my mom being my mom. When I was a kid, she was very strict with me. I wasn't allowed to stay over at people's houses. If she set a time I needed to be home, then I *needed* to be home. As I got older, she paid attention to everything: who I was hanging out with and who the people I was hanging out with were hanging out with. If she knew they were having sex or experimenting with drugs or doing anything she didn't approve of, I couldn't spend time with them. That was that. She was very conscientious and noticed every little thing, but I was never particularly angry about it. Looking back, I think it's beautiful that despite how busy my mother was in her own life, she was ever-present in mine, and I know that deep down I felt the same way back then. No kid wants a strict parent, but I wasn't bitter. I knew that her strict nature—what some might describe as overprotectiveness—was born of her wanting an easier life for me than the one she had. From the day I was born she wanted something different for me, and she started steering me in that direction from the moment she laid eyes on me.

As I got older though, my mom began to realize that the best lesson she could teach me was about how to take care of myself. We've always been close, and I know there have been times when she could see me making mistakes. Still, she always let me learn the hard way because she knew that was the only way the lesson would stick. And even when I was a teenager, she was clear that she was not going to handle anything for me that I should be able to handle myself.

When I was around fourteen, I told my mom that I wanted to go on a date. "A boy asked me out," I said, "can I borrow money for dinner?"

"If you don't have any money then you don't have any business going on a date!" my mom replied. She wasn't going to take care of me in that moment, and she wasn't going to let me rely on some teenage boy to take care of me, either. She provided for me when I needed it, but as I got older my mom made sure I shifted from being the fragile baby I once was to a young woman who could stand on her own two feet. If I wanted anything extra, that was on me. She never gave me the bread. Sometimes she would say, "You come up with half, I'll pay half," but she instilled in me a hustle mentality from the jump. I got my first job at fifteen, working at McDonald's, because I wanted to get my learner's permit, and the only way to do so was to go to driver's ed class, and that wasn't free.

My mom could be tough, but she was always supportive. When I was around nineteen, I started dating a woman. I hadn't even known that I was attracted to women, but the first time I saw

Ebony, at a club outside of Phoenix, Arizona, where we lived at the time, I was completely mesmerized. I thought she was beautiful, and I was certain I wanted to know more of her. Ebony and I started hanging out a lot, and then dating "officially;" I found that everything moved faster when I was in a relationship with a woman. I don't know if that's because we could connect differently emotionally or we knew what the other would like physically, but it was as if, one week in, we were already in love. It totally turned me out. But my mom and I were close, and I still lived at home. She wasn't strict with me, exactly, but she liked to know where I was and when I would be back, and I knew she was curious about this mystery person with whom I was spending all my time. And I did want to share the information with her, but I was also incredibly scared. I knew it might be tricky for my mom—it would be the first time she'd encountered one of her kids in a same-sex relationship. But hiding wasn't in my nature, and we didn't really keep secrets from each other.

One afternoon, my mom and I went on a shopping trip, and had parked sort of far away. For whatever reason, I felt like this was my moment. As we walked to Nordstrom Rack, I brought it up.

"Mom, I know you know I've been seeing someone, and I'm really starting to like them," I said. "I want to tell you . . . she's a girl."

My mother did a double take. "Wait, what?" she asked. "This is how you tell me? In the Nordstrom Rack parking lot?"

Clearly my mother was taken aback, and I could tell the

news wasn't exactly easy for her to swallow. She had some of the expected questions—*Is this a phase? Are you just experimenting? Or is this for real?*—and I answered honestly. I didn't think it was a phase, and I really liked this person. Once she heard what I had to say, she had only one last question. "When can I meet this human?" It came from a beautiful place.

Ebony and I were only together for a few months—not all that long in the scheme of things—but she did come over for Thanksgiving, and everyone treated her well. I was a nineteen-year-old exploring her sexuality and trying to figure herself out, and I was lucky to have a mother who allowed me that freedom. She didn't judge me or try to talk me out of it or tell me my feelings were unnatural. She wanted to me to have space to figure out who I was, without any shame, and that mattered. I think it brought us even closer, because it proved to her that I would always be honest, and it proved to me that my happiness was what mattered to her.

Still, as much as she rooted for my happiness, my mother was not about to manufacture it. She trained me to find my way on my own. I would need to be responsible for myself. That meant understanding the value of work and making money, and understanding that the real world would happen around me. There would be plenty I couldn't control, whether it was other people's behavior or my own physical ailments or cultural or political moments that were happening in society at large. The only thing I could count on for certain was myself. It wasn't a tough-love, you're-alone-in-this-world lesson but rather a you're-a-strong-woman, you-have-all-the-tools-you-need one. And it stuck with me. For better and for worse.

My life has never been easy. Not from the moment I was conceived. Life wasn't easy for my mother either. Or any of my ancestors. Perhaps that's why easy doesn't even appeal to me. I don't consider my success or the life I live today as something that happened *despite* hardship. I see it as something that happened *because* of the hardship.

I say my entry into the world was gnarly, but it set me on a path that I am nothing but grateful for. My mother always told me that life had something important in store for me, and she knew it would be greater than whatever storms I was forced to battle along the way. It didn't make the hard times easier (and, as you'll soon see, there were plenty of hard times), but it did infuse them, in some small measure, with purpose. There was a reason for every difficulty, even if I couldn't see it in the moment.

I wouldn't see it for a while, actually, but isn't that always the way?

Chapter Two

The Soul Instinct

It started with a tingle.

I was home with my two brothers on a Saturday afternoon, sitting on the floor of the living room, watching an episode of *The Flintstones* and eating ramen noodles, when a strange feeling began to trickle up the left side of my body. I was twelve years old, and by then we were living in Phoenix, Arizona, and had been there a couple of years.

My family moved from Virginia to Maryland when I was about six years old, and my mom got a job with a construction company working as an on-site nurse. She would call rescue workers if something happened, file accident reports, that sort of thing. On one job site they were installing a subway system, and they would check the water levels every day to see how deep they could dig. But one day, after checking, they left the manhole covers open. A worker fell off a scaffold and ten feet down into the ground. They blew the bullhorn to alert everyone that there was an emergency, but it was my mom's responsibility to run and call rescue. Well, it was a cold and icy day in Maryland, and as my mother bolted up the hill to the trailer to make the call, she slipped and she too fell into a manhole. It was a rough fall. She went four and a half feet down, tore up her back and her left knee, and ended up temporarily paralyzed on her left side. She didn't walk for a whole year.

Remember when I said that woman is a warrior? I wasn't kidding.

My mother's recovery was slow and grueling. It took three surgeries on her spine, but she was eventually able to walk. That in itself felt like a victory. Still, the unpredictable Maryland weather made everything harder—she had a metal rod in her back, and whenever it rained or the barometric pressure dropped, her bones ached. A warmer climate would make life more comfortable for her, her doctor said. Around the same time, one of my mom's girlfriends moved to Phoenix. She came back east for a visit and raved about life in Arizona—the dry heat, the relaxing pace . . . and did she mention the dry heat? My mom was intrigued. She went to Phoenix for a week, came home, and announced immediately that we were moving. It happened quick. None of us were happy to leave, but a month later we had packed up our lives and were headed west.

Back when we lived in Virginia, my mother had met and married a man named Frank. I was about five when they got together, and he had a son named Frankie, who became a second brother to me. Skip is my half brother—we have the same mom but different fathers—and we had lived together from the day I got home from the hospital as a baby. He is hilarious, always the life of the party. Today we're close, but growing up we had the typical brother-sister dynamic, fighting one minute, laughing together the next. Frankie and Skip are both six years older than me, so when Frankie arrived, the two of them became a pair. I was the younger kid who always wanted to tag along on their adventures, and they'd try to shake me and do their own thing. Still, we were a family, and when my mom said it was time to go, the five of us—my mom and stepdad, me, Skip, and Frankie—moved to Arizona. My uncle Stevie ended up staying with us too. We rented a few different places, but ultimately ended up in a house on a cul-de-sac where we stayed for a few years.

But back to the living room, where I was eating and watching TV. My left side began to tingle, and as I took notice of this strange feeling, I was confronted with two images that even then I knew weren't of this world. It was as if two spirits were standing in front of me, one black and one white. When I say black and white, I'm not talking about race. These were not people, or shapes of people. It was almost as if two orbs appeared before me, one emanating a black light, the other a white one. I didn't really know what I was dealing with, but when you're a twelve-year-old and you start having visions that are as vivid and clear as any human who has ever stood before you, you take notice.

So here I was, having this weird feeling in my left side, and now seeing things. The messages came next: The black-and-white visions told me that I was going to be OK, but that I was about to go through something really hard and really scary. My mom and dad were at the store, but they would be home soon, the spirits said, and when they were, they needed to know to take me to the hospital. "Your dad won't believe you, and that's OK. You just tell your mommy what we told you."

I had no idea what was going on, all I knew was that at this point I could barely feel the left side of my body. I wasn't scared, exactly, because I didn't know enough to be scared, but I was certainly weirded out. In fact, I think *because* I was so weirded out, I just went with it. I didn't have the wherewithal to question what was happening, maybe because it was all coming at me so fast. My brothers were home, so before I could even tell my mom, I told Skip what I saw. If I didn't know to be scared, he was terrified enough for the both of us. He was eighteen—old enough to look after me, but still basically a kid. Most of the time, looking after me meant turning on the TV and making sure the house didn't burn

The black-and-white visions told me that I was going to be OK, but that I was about to go through something really hard and really scary.

down. And here was his younger sister, talking about visions, with one half of her face paralyzed. I'm told that I then just sort of lay down on the floor, though I don't actually remember this. Skip knew something was very wrong, but it was the early 1990s: There were no cell phones; he couldn't call my mother and tell her to rush home. All we could do was wait.

Soon, as predicted, my mom and stepdad returned home. Skip ran outside to meet them before they could even make it out of the car.

"There's something wrong with Bea!" he said. "She said there was a white light and a black light, and now she's on the floor . . . and she's not faking."

"She's fine," my stepdad said. "She just wants attention." Frank didn't even wait to see me before dismissing my brother's claim. Before he and my mom had left the house, we'd all gotten in a fight. It was your typical kid stuff: I wanted to go out with friends and they didn't let me. There was no real reason for them to say no, at least none that my mother could point to, except the classic "because I said so." And even though it was my mom who said no first, I went to Frank next and asked the same thing, because I wanted to do what I wanted to do and going to the other parent was the oldest trick in the book. But he was not going to be fooled. "You heard your mom," Frank said. "The answer is no."

When they left the house, I was pouting. I was pissed that my mom wouldn't let me go see my friends and that I was stuck sitting at home, but she was not moved. "We'll talk about it when I get back," she said. So when they got back and pulled into the garage and Skip told them I was on the floor, Frank was unconvinced. I can't say I blame him—it would have been a good protest, if I'd had that in me. But this was not that. Luckily, my mom wasn't as quick to brush off my brother. She walked into the house, took one look at me, and knew that whatever was happening was very real. "This is not pouting," she said. "Something is not right." One side of my body was limp, and I was trying to talk to her but the words were coming out all garbled. She didn't know what was going on, but she knew *something* was going on, and no matter how angry I was to miss hanging out at a friend's house, she knew I simply wasn't that good of a faker.

My mom scooped me up and ran me into the car. By the time she was pulling out of the garage, I was having a full-blown stroke, and she was freaking out. I mean, here was her baby girl, having a stroke in her backseat. A baby who'd already been through her share of health problems, no less. As any mom probably would, my mother was driving like a maniac. Again! This was apparently a theme of my childhood. She was cruising on sidewalks and flying through red lights.

Most of that ride is a blur to me now, but a single moment stands out. We were at a stoplight, and my mom, this time, was waiting for the light to turn green. As we sat there, whatever spirit voice had warned me that I was about to go through a scary episode was now telling me, "You need to go right now.

Right now." I didn't know who or what these voices were, but they were loud and clear. Luckily, they were also not shy about assuring me that I would be OK. Of course, that's not so easy to believe when you're twelve years old and going through a traumatic medical event. I was terrified, and seeing the wild way my mom was driving didn't help.

Somehow my mother got me to Banner Thunderbird Medical Center without getting pulled over. She didn't even turn the car off, just rushed me into the hospital, telling anyone who would listen that something was happening to her baby and that she needed immediate help. It turned out that not only was I having a stroke but shortly after we arrived at the hospital I had a seizure, and then went into cardiac arrest.

Soon I was in a hospital room full of doctors and nurses, and my mother was waiting outside while the medical professionals were focused on getting the situation under control. While she waited, she called her Aunt Beazy, who had raised her since she was a child. "Call Aunt Jeni," Beazy told my mom. "She'll know what to do." When my mother tells this story today, she always wonders what made her listen in that moment. What woman, when her adolescent daughter is having a stroke and seizure and going into cardiac arrest, calls to check in with her aunt? From a pay phone no less! But she listened to Beazy, and when she got her aunt on the phone, Jeni was very clear: "Bea is going through the passage," she said.

Jeni was an intuitive, like many of the women in my family.

She believed in herbs more than medicine, and she was always using her various potions to heal herself and her family members. What Jeni meant about "the passage" was that I was receiving the gifts that had blessed my ancestors before me. I was coming into my ability to connect with the dead. But my mother wasn't interested in hearing about a damn passage, especially not while her baby was in danger. She was hysterical. I was sick, and all she cared about was making sure I was OK. She barely could put a sentence together on the phone. "You need to calm down," Aunt Jeni said. "If you go into that room and Bea sees you upset, then she'll get upset. Go in there and get the doctor on the phone—I need to talk to him."

My mom walked into my hospital room and approached the ER doctor, Dr. Burns. "Excuse me, my aunt needs to speak with you," she said. You can imagine how well that went over. He was dealing with a twelve-year-old under cardiac arrest. Dr. Burns looked at my mother like she had lost her mind.

"I'm in the middle of something here," he said.

"I understand that," my mom said. "But this is my child, and you must get on the phone with my aunt."

To Dr. Burns's credit, he listened to my mom. At that point I was coming out of the cardiac arrest and was stabilizing, so he took a moment and came to the phone.

Jeni quickly introduced herself to Dr. Burns, explaining that she was Native American and that ours was a deeply spiritual and connected family. "I don't need you to understand, but I do need you to listen," she said. "My niece is going through a rite of passage. You should give her a saline IV, but don't give her anything else. Trust me. That baby girl is going to be fine and you should not overmedicate her. She isn't sick."

"Ma'am, I am a medical doctor, and I will do what I need to do and what's best for my patient," Dr. Burns said. It was a reasonable reaction.

"Believe me," Aunt Jeni said, "all things will become normal soon. She is going through her veil."

Going through your veil, in spiritual speak, means that you are passing through a barrier. This moment was my initial experience connecting with the other side. It basically eliminated the separation between the living and nonliving world, so that I could communicate with spirits just as I could with living humans. But it happened so powerfully that it literally made me sick.

Obviously my doctor couldn't change his treatment plan based on the words of a stranger on the other end of the phone line, not to mention the fact that he didn't know what the hell a veil was, but the truth was that he didn't have much of a treatment plan yet. The doctors didn't know why I'd had the stroke or the seizures, so for the time being, their only real plan was to wait. Then, while he was talking to Jeni, a nurse from my room came into the hallway.

"Excuse me, Doctor, but she's fine now," the nurse said. "She's totally normal."

Everyone in that room had seen me go into cardiac arrest. It had happened before their eyes.

"What do you mean she's normal?" he said. "She can't be."

"I know, but she is." There was nothing more this nurse could say—my mom could tell she could barely believe it herself.

Dr. Burns returned to my room with my mom and saw that what the nurse said was true. My vitals were normal, and I was coming back into my regular consciousness.

"What happened?" I asked, in the meager voice of a kid who'd just been through the wringer.

Dr. Burns asked me the day of the week (Saturday) and my first and middle name (Beatrice Nikka) and if I had any numbness in my fingers or toes (no). He decided to keep me for observation for a few days and run a bunch of tests, but, to his credit, since he couldn't point to any clear cause of my health scares, he respected Aunt Jeni's request, which my mother had reiterated, and put me on only a saline IV. The nurses probably thought he was crazy, but he was a special man like that. He may not have understood what my aunt told him, but he didn't turn away from it, either.

For the next three days, it seemed like I went through every test imaginable, but nothing came up. "I've never seen anything like this," Dr. Burns said. (This was becoming a common refrain from my childhood doctors.) "We were all in that room, we saw what happened, but these tests are showing no sign of it."

When I was discharged, Dr. Burns attributed my episode to

a growth spurt—at least that's what he wrote in the paperwork. I shot up so quickly that my system couldn't handle it, he said. I don't know if he actually believed that, but he couldn't exactly credit "Native American rite of passage," which is what my aunt Jeni had told him. He did put me on Tegretol, an anti-seizure medication, in hopes of preventing any future episodes. "I went along with what your aunt suggested, and I'm glad it worked out," he told my mother. "But as a medical professional it's my job to make sure Bea's on proper meds and that we do what we can to prevent this from happening again." My mother asked if that's what he expected—a repeat episode—and he was honest that he couldn't say. He'd never seen a case like mine before, so he couldn't predict what would happen next.

I did end up having one more seizure. It was about a month later, and I was getting ready for school. It was still the beginning of the school year—I remember being excited to wear my new outfit when I felt the seizure coming on. Because I'd already been through this not long before, I recognized the signs enough to warn my mom it was happening again. We went to the ER, but by the time we got there the episode had passed and the doctors couldn't pinpoint what triggered it. They weren't particularly concerned, though, and just told me to follow up with Dr. Burns, which we did. He kept me on the Tegretol for another couple months, but I never had another seizure, and I was weaned off the meds pretty quickly. "The best judge of how Beatrice is doing is Beatrice," Dr. Burns told my mom. "She's the best monitoring system we have. If she says she's good, then she's good, and if she's not she'll let you know." He made sure I knew what to do if I felt a seizure coming on—get my mom, and then get low to the ground—but beyond that he was willing to admit that he didn't know everything about the human brain, and some things were beyond medical knowledge. It takes a good doctor to admit that some things are simply a mystery. I think he liked seeing something new, and being reminded that he had more to learn.

After that first episode, my life changed—I started to see things that others couldn't. I'd go to a friend's house and be able to sense that someone in the room was going to get sick. If I bumped into someone on the street, I could see pieces of their life playing like a movie in my mind. It was as if what happened on that monumental Saturday had opened a vortex, and now I could see moments from the future as if they were happening in front of me. It sounds scary, and maybe it was at first, but I didn't fully understand what was going on, or that it was particularly strange. It was just a part of me.

The moment of passage brought on by my stroke didn't just gift me with the ability to see the beyond—it also introduced me to my spirit guides, those ancestors and friends and even some beings that have never even come to this world, that watch over me and advise me. Most are my descendants, but some are family in spirit rather than blood, and others are simply the souls of individuals I admire. I'm not saying that what happened that day wasn't a real medical episode, because I had a stroke and a seizure and went into cardiac arrest in a short window. Those are serious health scares. I don't make light of them. In fact, I have a lot of trouble remembering the specifics of most memories from my childhood, and I tend to think that has something to do with the stroke and seizures. Maybe something inside me short-circuited, so to speak. I can't be sure. But I absolutely believe that these episodes were caused not by any ailment or illness but by the opening of a portal, something that bound me to the ancestors and guides and guardian angels that walk with me today.

Although the stroke and seizure episode forever connected me to those beyond the veil, I am not a practicing medium. I am, however, always in tune with the energy around me, and that connection has only sharpened as I've gotten older. These days, if there is a presence in the vicinity that wants to be known, whether it's someone to whom I'm personally connected or not, I can sense it, and I can make a choice to engage or not. As a kid, I wasn't quite there yet. I couldn't say "not today, thank you" to a spirit if it appeared. Still, it wasn't like they were coming to me on a consistent basis. My upbringing was not a whole *Sixth Sense* "I see dead people" situation. But I did have an ability to sense what was coming, almost as if I could see the future.

My mom told Dr. Burns about all of this. He'd earned our trust and respect, so we knew he wouldn't write us off as plain out of our minds.

"She can see what's going to happen as if she's looking at moving chess pieces," my mom said. "Is there any possible medical explanation?"

"Well, it's new to me, but she's a new one to me," he said. "If she says she sees it, I can't say she doesn't."

Then he'd turn to me and say, "Am I going to win the lottery today, Beatrice?"

"I don't see it, Dr. Burns," I'd say. He always got a real kick out of that.

To my family's credit, they didn't make much of a fuss about my visions or my ability to connect with our ancestors. It was a family gift, after all. Most of the women in my lineage can do the same, so it's not weird to us. I didn't grow up feeling "different," even if in retrospect I probably was. As far as I could see, I lived a pretty normal teenage existence. I didn't love school, but I locked into the activities I was passionate about. I had a group of friends, mostly the Black crowd, because there weren't a lot of us in my high school, so it was comforting to hang out with the kids who looked like me. I wasn't super popular, but I didn't particularly care to be. I wanted to do my time and move on. And while my mom was strict about who I could hang with or where I was allowed to go, she didn't insist on straight A's or give me a hard time about schoolwork. *Take it seriously and do the best you can.* That was her motto, and I appreciated that, because it allowed me to direct my energy to the activities I was good at and had fun with. I've never been someone who can excel without passion. Just going through the motions is not my MO. I don't enjoy academia and I never did—it never came naturally to me—but I joined the Future Business Leaders of America and DECA (both are organizations for students interested in entrepreneurship) and played basketball. I had some gifts, but I would say that all kids do. My connections to the beyond were not the main focus of my life, but rather a piece of myself that I simply accepted as fact.

Mostly, my spirits made themselves known in the pivotal moments of my life. They came when I was having the stroke and seizure, and then from time to time in adulthood, especially in hard moments or when I was at a crossroads. And while I absolutely believe this is a gift, I don't think of myself as some sort of "chosen one." We all have guardian angels who travel with us through our lives, whether we are conscious of them or not. Some of us choose to believe this fact, others choose not to—but I believe that my awareness and faith in my spirituality is what differentiates me from most people more than any actual psychic ability.

Still, as I matured, so did my ability to tap into my gifts. When it first started, visions would appear, but I wasn't particularly in control of the moment. I saw what was in front of me, but it was as if the vision was happening *to* me, pouring in like rain through an open window. I was almost a witness to these visions, a bystander. Sometimes I was barely even aware they were happening until after the fact—I could intimate that there was a certain energy in the air, but I wasn't aware, in the moment, of what exactly was going on. And, because I was young, I couldn't always interpret what I saw. At a friend's house I might say "Mommy, we have to leave, there's an accident coming," but I couldn't go so far as to say to my friend, "You are going to get in an accident soon, be careful." That changed as I got older. First of all, I didn't live with my mother. We've always been close, but once I was grown, I was grown, and I couldn't always turn to her to interpret what was coming at me. I couldn't rely on her to do the work that I needed to do. I also *wanted* to be responsible for my own gifts. And again, it wasn't like I was seeing the future every day. But there were moments, and I began to have a better sense of them.

Consider this: You can't remember the first time you felt love, right? It's just a part of you. For me, connecting with my ancestors is the same thing. There were moments when it freaked me out, and some when I didn't really have any feelings about it at all. I accepted it as a fact of my life because my mom told me it was—the same way a kid might accept they have a peanut allergy because their mom told them as much. It didn't define me, and I didn't want to give it that much attention because I wanted to be a normal kid. It was just there. The same way my love for my family was just there. I didn't think about where it came from, or question its veracity. I mostly ignored it. But now, as an adult, I find it comforting—it's a beautiful thing to be able to commune; there is a safety in knowing that spirits are watching and protecting me from the other side. It took time for me to get there, but today I am so grateful to have been blessed with this ability and to come from a lineage that has handed this down to me.

Not everyone is so receptive to connecting with the dead, of course. As my life has evolved, so have my gifts, and it's not just my own ancestors and guides that appear anymore. Sometimes

I'll be in a room with someone—it could be an acquaintance or friend, it could be a complete stranger—and a spirit will pull up. I can sense them in the room. You know when you're in, say, a coffee shop, and you can feel someone looking at you? Or when you think you're alone in your home, but you suddenly get the sense that someone else is there? That's what this feels like. I can sense another presence. It's not as creepy as when I can feel someone staring, necessarily, but it's that similar sensation. I just know I'm not alone. And the presence that is with me, they know that I know I'm not alone.

When I first started doing Reiki, my healer told me that I needed to spend more time with my inner child. This is what he felt from me, he said. I still had to heal from moments in my past. But inner-child work is hard for me. I've heard from friends that when they want to do work on their inner child, they like to envision themselves in their most vulnerable young moments and tell that child that everything will turn out OK. That they will grow up to be a therapist, or a mom, or a teacher, so they can say, *See, we are going to be OK. All will end up as it should.*

The idea of that kind of reassurance has always sounded nice to me, but actually practicing it is much harder. When someone talks to me about my inner child, I immediately think back to that day in my living room in Phoenix—the white and black lights that warned me that a scary moment was coming. It might have been an important opening for me, but in the moment, twelve-year-old Bea didn't feel in control. She felt scared, and I don't particularly like reliving that moment, even when I know that it all turned out OK. I haven't wanted to experience that again. I told Keon, my Reiki healer, that I don't love inner child work, but also that my childhood as a whole is unusually hard for me to remember. As I've said, I think that's due to the stroke and seizure and the medical stuff, but because those episodes were so scary, tapping into my inner child brings about a lot of emotion—enough so that I tend to avoid it.

Keon heard me, and he respected it, but as we began to work together more often and talk about this more, I opened up a bit. One day I showed up for our Reiki session and decided to tell him all about the day of the stroke. He listened, and simply said, "Let's just go there right now, I'll sit with you as we revisit, so it doesn't have to be so scary." I was wearing black leggings and a white T-shirt. He sat me down and helped me go back to that moment. I saw myself as a young girl, and I sat down with that girl and told her, *You are going to be OK, but you are about to go through something really hard and really scary. Your dad won't believe you,* I said. *And that's OK. You just tell your mommy what we told you.*

Suddenly, it hit me. Those two visions I had all those years ago—the black light and the white light? They weren't two separate beings. They were *me*. Forty-year-old Bea, in her black leggings and white T-shirt, coming to assure her younger self that she was going to be OK. *I was the spirit.* I had traveled back in time, to look out for young Bea. It wasn't only my ancestors who saved me. I saved myself.

I always say that all things are in order. Life happens as it should—because of how my gifts unfolded, I was not only able to sit with my younger self and tell her everything was going to be OK, but I had a chance to warn her, so that she could tell her brother, who would tell her mother, who would get her to the hospital. Who knows what would have happened if, for example, when I was twelve, I hadn't told Skip what was happening. I might not have gotten to the hospital quickly enough; I might have been in the car when I went into cardiac arrest rather than in a hospital surrounded by medical professionals. To be in a place where you can be open enough and present enough to sit down with yourself in the past, to be your own savior—that is a gift. And to realize this, to know that not only are those from the beyond watching over me, but that I am always helping myself? It reminds me that I am going to be OK. Even in that moment when I am no longer in this body because my spirit is going back home, I know it will be a

To be in a place where you can be open enough and present enough to sit down with yourself in the past, to be your own savior—that is a gift.

beautiful transition, because there is more than this one body for my soul. And I know that when I am in a jam, I can call on my spirit guides and my ancestors and also myself from past lives and future ones to get what I need. It doesn't mean I will get handed all the answers—I know for certain that I won't—but having the answers isn't the goal. The journey is in the seeking. I feel lucky to know that even when I'm doing that alone, I'm in good company.

Chapter Three

You Have to Get Lost to Find Your Way

"Whatever you do in life, you will be very successful," Kelly, my first full-time boss, said to me.

I was nineteen, and we were sitting in her office in the back of the Cigna pharmacy, where she had just offered me my first-ever promotion. I was young, but I was getting an early glimpse of what Career Bea could look like.

I'd been working at the pharmacy for a year at that point. After graduating high school, I enrolled in community college, where I was briefly pre-med, mostly because my mom always wanted me to be a doctor. She knew I was a healer, so she liked the idea of making that official. She had worked in the hospital system as a biller, so she knew a lot of people there. Kelly was a friend of hers—a pharmacist who, at the time, needed an assistant—so my mom got me an interview. I wasn't particularly passionate about pharmacy work, but I knew how to sell myself. I knew how to talk to people. Kelly, a short white woman with glasses who was kind but also all business, hadn't planned on giving me the job—the interview was nothing more than a favor for a friend—but we clicked. I think I might have reminded her of herself. I didn't know what I wanted to do with my life or where exactly to direct my hustler mentality, but I knew I wanted to work hard. I deeply craved success and independence. I had an entrepreneurial spirit, even if I couldn't name it at the time, and Kelly could see that. I made clear to her that when I had a job to do, I didn't mess around. I was driven, and she must have recognized that, because something about our conversation inspired her to take a chance on me.

I liked the work—I was helping to allocate and dispense medications, learning about formulations, and interacting with customers—and I worked hard. This was my first real job as an adult and I took it seriously. I didn't procrastinate or get distracted. I did what was asked of me and when I didn't understand I asked for help. That didn't seem especially noteworthy to me at the time—how are you going to figure something out if you don't ask?—but I know now that plenty of teenagers don't operate that way. What I knew then was that I was eighteen years old and making $25 an hour. That was a lot, and I didn't want to screw it up.

I loved feeling successful in that job, but just as meaningful was that my boss saw potential in me. I hadn't experienced a lot of that. It's one thing to get hyped up by your mom, but it was easy to write that off as *she's my mom, she has to encourage me.* My doctors might have called me a miracle child, but I didn't earn that title. Not really. It wasn't for actually *doing* anything. In school, teachers didn't take any special interest in me, because I didn't take any special interest in them or what they were offering. I could not get out of high school fast enough. I went to school and did my best, because I didn't feel I had a choice, but the day I got my senior yearbook, I returned it for a refund. No disrespect to any of my classmates, but I knew I was never going to look at that thing again, and I was never going to see any of those people again. I wasn't bullied or picked on, I just wasn't interested. My goal was to pass my courses so that I could be done and get on with my life.

Community college wasn't all that different. I dropped out after a semester, because, like I said, school just wasn't for me. I'm more of an on-the-job learner, and Kelly couldn't believe my work ethic. Or my curiosity. I didn't just do what I was told. I sought out more work. I really wanted to understand each part of the pharmacy—how to compound, how to work IVs—so any time there was an opportunity for me to do that, I jumped on it, and Kelly appreciated it. She had no reason to invest time or energy in me if she didn't think it would pay off, but she saw that I had a future, and now she was encouraging me to get my pharmacy tech certification. The only problem—and it was a big one—was that I knew I couldn't stay there. I didn't want to be in Phoenix.

Despite the fact that I had embarked on a career, I was really still a kid. I may have had drive and potential, but I had barely ever tasted real freedom. I still lived at home! I deeply believed I was destined for success one day, but I had a lot of learning to do in terms of what success looked like, or how to get there. I'd wanted to move back to Maryland pretty much since the moment my family arrived in Arizona. Phoenix is not an especially diverse city. I never really saw myself in the people there, and that was hard for me. I'd spent the first decade of my life in the Maryland/DC area, so other than Phoenix it was all I really knew. If I could just make it back there, I thought, I'd be around more humans of color and my life could finally begin. I thought I would have more opportunity to thrive. I was willing to work really hard to achieve my dreams, but I needed to be in a place where opportunities existed for people who looked like me, and I just didn't see much of that in Phoenix. So despite the fact that my life was developing at a good clip—I had a job and a boss who saw potential in me—I decided to move back East.

As it turned out, my time in Maryland was a short-lived experiment. I moved there with no job, just the idea that it had to be better than Arizona. I had no place to live, so I crashed for a bit with my mom's aunt and her two kids. I love them dearly to this day, and my mom's aunt treated me well—she fed me and watched out for me—but I couldn't find work, and life was not falling into place for me under their roof. After a few months I moved in with my godmother, who lived in a nicer neighborhood, and I got a job answering phones at a garage door company. Still, after about a year I looked around at what my life had become, and all I could think was, *This isn't it.* I was nineteen, finally an adult, and here I was staying in other people's houses and totally dependent on them, which was the opposite of the independence I was looking for. Plus, I was driving an hour a day to get to work, which may not sound so bad, but it's not how you want to spend your time at nineteen years old. Honestly, it was terrible. I never established any friendships there and I knew almost immediately upon arriving that I'd made a mistake. I was young and I'd held on to this idea of what life in Maryland would be, if only I could get back there, and now I was learning that memories have filters. The real Maryland could never live up to what I'd created in my mind, and that move didn't give me what I'd thought it would. I wasn't happy and I knew I couldn't stay. I didn't want to return to Phoenix, but I also didn't see what choice I had.

Back at home, my mom never said the words "I told you so" but . . . she told me so. She knew I was making a mistake when I left home, that I had built Maryland up in my mind, but she also knew that she had to let me go out into the world and come to that realization on my own. Now here I was, only a year or so later, back in her house. I was back to working at Cigna. It felt like things were never going to change, but at least this time

I was a little bit older and a little bit wiser. Everyone needs a second chance—or even a third or fourth—and I knew I needed a reset after the unsuccessful Maryland stint. I needed to chill and be taken care of. It's not like my mom had a lot of money, but being with her felt safe and comfortable. And yet I also still craved excitement and freedom. I know now that those feelings—safety and comfort and excitement and freedom—can coexist. You don't have to choose. But I didn't get it back then.

For the next couple of years, things went well enough in Phoenix. I was stacking a little bit of bread and I was able to get my own apartment downtown. I left Cigna and got a job at the pharmacy of Banner University Medical Center. I was doing skin-care compounding and working in the IV room, and I was learning a lot and getting paid well. Eventually I was even made the manager of the night shift, and I was only in my early twenties! I could feel myself getting settled into life in Arizona, and usually that's a good thing, but it startled me. *If I stay here much longer, I'm going to* be *here*, I'd think to myself. I could see it so clearly, how a person starts a job with the intention of staying only until the next thing comes along, and ten years later she's looking around like, *Shit, I thought there was going to be a next thing.* It's not that there's anything especially bad about Phoenix. For a lot of people, it's a great city. But it just wasn't for me. Back then, Phoenix was not a place to be young, gifted, and Black. It's very suburban. You go to school, you get a job, you buy a house, you settle down. There wasn't really another way to live. It's monotonous, and I've been allergic to monotony since

I was a kid. Plus, I was young! At forty, a quiet, predictable life might sound calming or comforting. But at twenty-two? No. I had energy. I craved something new. Something different. Something exciting. I wanted to prove to myself that I could stand on my own two feet, in a city where I had no family to support me and no one to rely on but myself. I wanted to know that I could handle adulthood. I had about $800 saved, and I knew two things: I had to get out of Phoenix once and for all, and I couldn't move anywhere without a job. That much I'd learned, and I wasn't about to make the same mistake twice.

With this new plan in mind, I set my sights on New York and Atlanta. I hadn't been to either one, but I wanted big-city, urban energy. I wanted to have fun! I applied to jobs in both places and decided that wherever I got an offer, I would take that as a sign from the universe of where I was supposed to be. When Emory Healthcare in Atlanta called with an opening in their pharmacy department, I was ready. The minute I received that offer I knew I was on my way. Leaving was a no-brainer, and knowing that I had a paycheck waiting for me in Georgia made the move a whole lot easier.

I arrived in Atlanta in 2005. I had a job but no place to live. I had my $800 in my pocket. That wasn't no damn money! But I didn't care. I believed that whatever I needed, I would figure it out. If I'd had a life motto back then, that would have been it: *I'll figure it out.*

In Atlanta, I could see myself everywhere. My arrival aligned nicely with the heyday of the city's social scene. It was shortly after the arrest of the Black Mafia Family, and hip-hop culture was at its height. I quickly fell in with a cute crowd who knew how to have fun. It started with me and my friend Tasha. We had both moved to Atlanta from Phoenix, where we'd met at church, and were roommates in an extended-stay motel while we looked for a place to live. We ended up meeting another girl, Rachel, who worked as a leasing agent at the apartment complex where we ended up renting. Rachel was cool as shit, and the three of us became inseparable. If we weren't at her place, she was at ours. She also had a ton of friends in Atlanta, and they were the *it* crowd, so she was the source of all our fun.

Through that fun, I also met Simon, who became like a big brother to me. Simon was fun but responsible—he worked as a CPA—and became a source of stability for me. He was the guy I went to for advice, because the rest of us, well, we were having fun but we weren't exactly in a position to give any advice. We were going out five nights a week, Monday through Friday. The weekend wasn't the time to go out, that was the time for chilling. If you really partied, that happened on weekdays. We hit up strip clubs, dance parties, VIP sections—all of it. Some of the people I partied with had a lot of money—they'd buy a section at a club, or hand us a cup full of twenties to pass on to the dancers. We'd go to Magic City, the legendary strip club, every Monday. Yes, there were girls dancing, but my friends and I just treated it like any other club, another place to party. Tuesday nights the destination would change, same with Wednesdays and so on, but every night we knew where the party was, and we were out all hours. It was wild and maybe it wasn't the most responsible way to live, but it was a damn good time. That's what your twenties are for! I wasn't doing anything *that* crazy—no hard drugs—but I was smoking a lot of weed and drinking and making it rain in the clubs thanks to other people's money. I also did a lot of traveling. A friend would say "Let's go to Miami," and we wouldn't have a place to stay, wouldn't have much money to spend when we got there, but we'd go down to Florida and assume we'd figure it out. And we always did.

I know now that I was living recklessly. I was chasing what I *thought* freedom and fun should look like, but I was only going to learn that through experience. At the time, the only real problem I could see was exhaustion. I was partying all night, rolling into my apartment at 4 or 5 a.m., sleeping for an hour or two, and then getting up to go to work and do it all over again. I was expected to be at my day job by 8 a.m., and it was forty-five minutes away from my place, which meant I was subsisting on barely any sleep, and trying to catch up on the weekends. You might think this would have signaled to me that it was time to dial back the nightlife, but I was young and stupid and didn't see how good I had it. My takeaway was not to change the social life. My conclusion was that I was burned out on pharmacy work. I was also hanging out with a lot of people who worked for themselves and made their own money on their own terms. They had various jobs, but each of them had control over their schedule in a way that I didn't, but really wanted to. *I'm going to take my life into my own hands*, I thought. I didn't want to work for somebody else anymore, and I certainly didn't want to stop partying, so I decided to leave my day job. It was a decision I made on my own, but if I'd tried to go on like that much longer, I'm sure my boss would have made it for me. The people at my job weren't idiots—they could see that I was rolling in under-slept and underprepared. I wasn't showing up as my best self, and there was no hiding that. If I hadn't quit, I'm sure I would have been fired in short order.

I still needed to find a way to make rent, so it was time to tap into that entrepreneurial spirit. The first thing I did after leaving my day job was start a cleaning business. A friend of mine mentioned he needed someone to clean his house, and my first thought was, *Wait, I can do that.* Tasha and I posted an ad on Craigslist: $35 for a home cleaning. That's crazy cheap! We got a lot of calls from that ad. We would go in and clean these houses and make them sparkle from top to bottom. These clients had never seen their houses look so good. Then, when they asked us to come back again the next week, we would immediately raise the price. The $35 introductory deal was only a onetime thing.

We ramped up our business pretty quickly. Like any line of work, securing clients was largely about who you know. We were out at night, being cute, and we'd meet someone at a club and tell them what we did. We cleaned for a lot of different people, from drug dealers to NBA players, most of whom we met out at night—guys with money to burn who wanted cute girls coming into their homes. We also got connected with a real estate agent who was often hired to find rental properties for actors who were in town shooting films or TV shows with Tyler Perry Studios. She'd need the places cleaned and prepped for actors to stay, and she brought us a lot of business. Soon, one thing led to another. Something I've learned over decades of different jobs is that, no matter what you do, if you work hard enough, more opportunities will come your way. If you do a good enough job at cleaning, clients start to ask if you can do organizing. What about decorating Christmas trees? One client hired me to cook for him—I wasn't a chef by any means, but I could follow a recipe and put a dinner together, so I did. The business grew and kept us busy, but it wasn't a lucrative endeavor. We were always scrambling to earn our keep.

> We cleaned for a lot of different people, from drug dealers to NBA players, most of whom we met out at night—guys with money to burn who wanted cute girls coming into their homes.

As this was all happening, I continued to frequent the strip clubs when I was out partying. I began to notice just how much money the girls who danced there were making. They were working their asses off, that was obvious, but hard work never scared me. I began to wonder if I could give it a shot. I knew I could never do what the women at the poppin' clubs in Atlanta did—they were so talented that it was beautiful, almost mesmerizing, to watch—but at a smaller club? I thought maybe I could pull it off. I approached the house mom at one of the less popular spots that I sometimes visited. A house mom is the person who takes care of the girls at a club. She always has wipes and wash and lotion and body spray. She has perfume and chewing gum. She helps with extra outfits and makeup. The house mom is backstage, almost like a dressing-room manager, so she knows what it takes to dance and to make it at the club, and she can usually tell who is fit for the job and who is definitely not. I told her that I wanted a chance. I insisted that I could dance and perform and do what was necessary to make a living. "Why not?" she said. "Let's see what you can do." She wasn't directly in charge of hiring, but if she put in a good word for me, I knew I'd get the gig.

Everything I knew about dancing I'd learned from my time as a patron. Once I got the OK from the house mom, I went out and bought myself shoes and an outfit. What you wear as a stripper is not the same as the lingerie you might wear at home—it was more corsets and heels than lacy nightgowns—so I tried to make sure I looked the part. Then, on my first night, I showed up and hoped for the best. I figured I'd seen enough lap dances to know how to give one. I had a sense of what worked with the clientele. But the first couple of nights, I won't lie, it was hard as hell. They would call my name up to the stage, and I was so intimidated. I didn't know how to do the pole, and I certainly didn't have the body strength for it, so I didn't even try. I was just trying to dance on stage. But even doing that, all by myself in front of a crowd, was scary. Not afraid-for-my-life scary, but certainly all-eyes-are-on-me scary. And sure, I know how to dance, but I'm not a Dancer. I just got out there and tried my best to be sexy. I crawled around on the floor and held on to the pole without trying to hoist myself up. I probably looked as awkward as I felt. Everything about it screamed new kid in town.

As the nights went on, I got a little bit more comfortable. Each evening was a little less terrifying. Still, when you're dancing at a strip club, you're working for tips. I was not getting an hourly wage. And most of the time I wasn't up on the stage. I was walking around, trying to catch someone's eye who might want to call me over for some company. I learned quickly that most of the time, the humans that go to these places, they just want to talk. There is a sexual aspect to it, for sure, but some people just want a chance to be heard. Some of them are unhappy at home. Plenty of them are lonely. I didn't have to break my back to get paid. I just had to walk around and be cool, so that I'd be invited to sit with someone. When I was, I'd just say, *How are you? What's your life like? Do you want a dance?*

It was my job to show an interest in the club's patrons, but most of the time I didn't care what these people had to say. A part of me always felt a little bit unsafe. I was in a desperate situation surrounded by other people in their own desperate situations. I had a couple of regulars who were there almost every night, but I wasn't looking to learn their life story and I was certainly not focused on their hardships. I had my own life to deal with! Of course, that didn't matter. I had to sit there and listen if I wanted to collect my tips and make a living. And frankly, giving one lap dance wasn't going to get me there. A single dance would earn me twenty bucks, and I had to give a portion of that to the house. The only real way to make any money was either to get a lot of regulars or to get invited into a VIP room for a private dance. If you want to earn good money, you're constantly selling yourself.

One night, about a month into working at the club, I was having a rough time. I just wasn't making any money, and my rent was coming due. I locked eyes with a guy who was there with a woman—I still don't know if she was his wife or his girlfriend. He signaled for me to come over and sit with them, so I headed in their direction. They were a bit older than me, probably in their early thirties. We started talking, and I wasn't sitting with them for long before they suggested we go to a VIP room. That was great news for me, because while a lap dance is $20, a private dance is more like $200.

And still, I was nervous. I was relatively new at the job, and I didn't really know what I was getting into. After all, the VIP room really is private. There are security guards standing outside the door, so I knew that if something went terribly wrong and I screamed, someone would hear me. But even if it didn't get to that point—and I didn't expect that it would—you can't know what's going to happen when you enter an intimate space with a couple of strangers you know nothing about.

The three of us headed to a back room, and I began dancing for the man. But he wanted me to dance for his partner, so I moved in her direction. Eventually, I was dancing for both of them.

"What are you doing after this?" the guy asked me as I stood between them. "Do you want to come home with us?"

I hadn't given much thought to going home with clients yet. But I knew that even the $200 I was getting for this private dance wasn't going to cut it for my rent after I paid the house their share. I knew that I needed to eat. I knew that I needed to pay for gas for my car and electricity for my apartment. I also knew, because she was always very up-front with me, that my mother had sold her body for a time when she needed to make ends meet. She worked in DC, with politicians and other high-profile clients, and made a hell of a lot more than I would make on this evening, but she had never hid that truth from me. You do what you have to in order to survive, and in this moment, I felt like I was grasping for survival.

This couple told me to name my price, so I came up with a number right then and there: $400. They didn't blink.

"Cool," they said. "Run it."

I went back to my locker and got dressed, and then I got in my car and followed this couple back to their house. I was at their place for no more than an hour, but it was long enough to have sex with each of them, make them come, collect my bread, wash up, and get out.

Sitting in my car, about to head home, I felt . . . off. I knew something had changed. Going home with that couple and giving them what they wanted—it was easy. In fact, it was way, way too easy. Dancing in front of a crowd? Now that was hard. That felt scary. But fucking a couple for money? It barely affected me. And the fact that it didn't affect me . . . *that's* what affected me. Four hundred dollars in less than an hour was the quickest and easiest money I'd ever made. But realizing just how easy it was, and how quickly it could become my livelihood, was a real wake-up call. I could probably do that again the next night, and the next, and my money problems would be over. But I also knew I didn't want that life.

Also, I wasn't dumb. I wasn't naïve. I knew that I got lucky. That evening could have turned out very differently. Those people could have done anything to me. And yet, because I was in a situation where I was acting out of desperation, I did something that could have put me in harm's way. I thought I'd been chasing freedom, but I found myself in free fall.

Okay, Bea, I thought, *your stripping days are over.*

I left their house and that was it. I never went back to that club again, never danced again, never again put myself in a circumstance where I was going home with a complete stranger.

Now, I want to be clear. I do not judge what anyone else does with their body. Plenty of people make their money with their bodies and I respect that. Wherever you are, be there. Survival is personal; making a living is personal; we all have the right to utilize our bodies as we see fit, and I have all the esteem in the world for any human who makes an honest living, no matter what their line of work. But that evening, with that couple? That was not in alignment with where I wanted my life to be and how I wanted to spend my time. And I'm not going to lie, there were a couple more times where I needed to make a buck and I found myself in sexual situations. There was this one guy, specifically, who a bunch of my friends knew, and he was into some kinky stuff. He would pay us to pee on him and to smell our panties. Sometimes there was an occasion where he did this with a bunch of women at once, and I'd be one of them. But he was harmless, and I wasn't fucking anybody, so when the opportunity popped up to pocket some extra cash, I took it. I thought it was weird, sure, but it was easy and I was in survival mode. Who was I to judge what he was into?

My dancing stint came and went. I did it for only about a month—the cleaning work lasted longer. Our business kept growing. But it was hard! Cleaning houses is really difficult work. First of all, it involves hours on your feet, doing physical labor. Also, there's no steady income. You make money when you clean, but there are no sick days. There's no paid vacation. If you don't show up one day, you don't get paid. You could be cleaning a house that's two thousand square feet or an apartment that's eight hundred square feet, and it can be filthy and disgusting, with toilets covered in shit and floors covered in hairballs, but what are you going to do? You have to eat. And even though I was working my ass off, cleaning and organizing and cooking and decorating Christmas trees, every day was a struggle. I appreciated being in charge of my schedule and owning my time and working for myself, but I hated that I couldn't rely on money in my bank account every two weeks. It's one thing to reject authority, a nine-to-five job, and stability for the freedom to pursue a big idea that lights your soul on fire. But cleaning was not that. I didn't actually care about the work; I did it because I had to. And I hated that no matter how hard I worked, I could never stay on top of my rising costs. That kind of stress is hard to live with, and it wears on a person. On their body. Their spirit. Their mind.

My roommate and I were always playing catch-up. Rent in Atlanta wasn't cheap, not to mention the cost of food and utilities. Plus, we were still partying most nights. We would go to the club with these men who would throw around a bunch of money, which I wanted them to do because I couldn't afford it for myself, but at the same time, I was sick of men taking advantage of me. I didn't want to have to wait on someone else to get into a club, and I didn't want anyone to feel like they owned me or that I owed them. These were not guys who had my best interests at heart; they just liked how I looked by their side, and a little piece of me died each time I had to rely on their dime, because it's not how I was raised. And yet, I was having fun. I don't want to say my priorities were out of whack, because here I am telling the story all these years later, but Tasha and I were not spending our money like responsible young adults who cared about paying our landlord on time. We were already robbing Peter to pay Paul, and eventually the inevitable happened. We got evicted.

For the next couple of months, we bounced around. We were lucky to have clients and friends who would look after us and let us crash on their couches, but we knew we couldn't ask that of them all the time, so we spent plenty of nights at the Motel Six or whatever establishment we could afford. We weren't sleeping on the street or in cars, but we didn't have any place to call home.

When people think of homelessness, it's easy to picture someone with no shoes or torn clothes sleeping under a bridge, or a family on a street corner asking for change. But the reality is very different—there are so many different versions of what it looks like to not have a permanent place to stay, and that stress is very real. Tasha and I were lucky to constantly run into kind people who would help us out, but it's scary and unnerving to continually wonder where you're going to sleep that night. It is stressful and traumatic and it's not something I would wish on anyone.

Eventually, one of our wealthier clients told us he had a big house off Moreland Avenue and he was searching for someone to look after it. This man let us stay in his home for about $1100 a month, which was cheap for any place, let alone for a giant house. He definitely could have gotten a lot more, and we were grateful.

Still, my mother's words, and the lessons she taught me, were always ringing in my ears. If I couldn't take care of myself,

I shouldn't be letting someone else do that work for me. If I couldn't pay a big city rent, what business did I have living in a big city? If I couldn't afford to go out partying, what was I doing every night? My friends and I used to go out on dates just so we could eat, and it was completely antithetical to everything I'd been told as a kid. I was raised by the woman who said "If you don't have any money, then you don't have any business going on a date!" That was ingrained in me from the time I was a kid! To be fair, the hustle mentality my mother instilled in me is what kept me afloat and helped me scrape by when I was living recklessly. I had to harness all the characteristics that would eventually serve me well in my career: a strong work ethic, creativity, calculated risk-taking, EQ, independence, and the soul instinct. Those traits are what saved me when things could have gone very badly.

But at the same time, I knew that this life of instability was not what my mother had in mind when she taught me to fend for myself. She did not raise me to be a woman who was always *this close* to the edge. Bouncing around and relying on the kindness of others just to get by? She worked too hard to secure a different life for me, and even in the haze of a wild young adulthood, I could see I wasn't honoring that. Also, this life was wearing me down! I was always chasing something or trying to prove something. I woke up one day and suddenly thought to myself, *What are you doing, girl? What are these decisions you're making? This is for the birds. It's stupid!*

The realization really did happen that quickly. What's funny is, even when I was running around partying, I was always someone who spent time thinking about how she wanted to live. I knew that my life and my actions were my responsibility. But I also knew I wanted to have a good time. This was my youth, and I wanted to make the most of it—at least until it stopped being fun. And eventually, that's what happened. There's only so much enjoyment you can get out of a life where you have so little stability. I lived it, and I loved it for a stretch, but I was *done.* I needed more structure and order to my days. I needed a change in my environment. I needed to take care of myself. I needed a steady job! Tasha and I had enjoyed ourselves and we'd done a lot of living and it was beautiful—it's a blessing to be able to come out of that life and look back on it and tell the stories and say I survived, but it was a crazy time, and I couldn't hack it anymore. I was tired of cleaning for people, and I couldn't keep working just to get by. I couldn't keep living in lack. I had quit my pharmacy job with this idea that I was going to take control of my existence and make something happen for myself, and instead I felt like my life was happening around me while I was hanging on by a thread. I wasn't being intentional. The way I wanted to live and the way I was living didn't match, and that wasn't working for me. I decided I wanted to live my life in alignment.

Of course, this was real life, not a fairy tale. You can decide you want to change your life, but nothing happens overnight. Still, I made some quick adjustments that helped to shift my direction. I decided to move out of our client's house and in with another old friend who I felt was living a quieter life. I couldn't stop cleaning because I needed the money and I had regular clients who relied on me, but I decided to look for a steady shift job, too, one with benefits and a reliable paycheck. I wanted to get my body right and my mind right.

At this point it was 2010, probably the height of Whole Foods' popularity. If you wanted to eat healthy or get herbal remedies or pursue an organic and natural route to health, Whole Foods was the spot. This was before every corner store and beauty company was pushing their own clean products, so when I found out that my local Whole Foods was hiring in its Whole Body section, it seemed like the perfect opportunity. Whole Body was the section of the store where the beauty products and supplements were sold. But like the food in the grocery section, these personal care products were free of artificial colors or flavors, and they largely used plant-derived and naturally derived ingredients. Whole Body was basically the drugstore section of Whole Foods, but it looked more like an apothecary. And because the products we sold were usually not the same mass-market products you would see at your regular grocery store, those of us in the Whole Body section needed to know our stuff. Customers were always asking for help or advice, and my background in pharmacy served me well.

All the people who worked at Whole Foods, as well as the people who shopped there, were trying to acquire knowledge about their bodies. That was the connective tissue of all the humans who roamed the aisles of that store—they wanted to feed their bodies, literally, with ingredients that would serve them. They wanted to take care of themselves, and I was finally in that same headspace. I knew that the way I'd been living—drinking all the time, smoking a lot of weed, doing ecstasy occasionally, skipping out on sleep—was not honoring my body. But at Whole Foods, at least back then (and maybe now too, I just don't know), they took care of their employees. They would send us on these health immersions—getaways where employees would sit in on educational sessions and eat healthy food and move our bodies and meet the people behind some of the most successful companies that we sold on our shelves. At the store, they'd have a whole team of medical doctors and nurses come in and do bloodwork and health exams and help you understand what was happening with your body. That was also how they determined your employee discount—the healthier you were, the bigger the discount. It incentivized me to get my physical health in check, and I appreciated that.

I was making moves in other parts of my life too. The most radical change was in my social life. I started to disconnect from a lot of the friends and relationships that had been a big part of my life over the last five years. You are who you hang with, I've always believed that, and no disrespect to my friends from that time, but I knew I didn't want to live like that anymore. The frequency with that group was too low for me now. It was all very superficial—everything was about partying and drugs and drinking, so unless somebody had money, we weren't talking to them. It was all about *what do you do, who do you know?* Nobody was looking for connections or deep relationships.

Everybody was out for theirs, and it was taking energy from me rather than giving. So I took a hard right. I made some friends at Whole Foods. I found the Afro house music scene, and I'd go to those parties and meet people who seemed to be living on a higher vibration than those I'd previously been hanging with. This new crowd, they had knowledge of themselves. They had respect for their bodies and their minds. They ate well. They were deeply spiritual. It seemed like they were tapped into a source, whereas the energy in the crowds that I used to run in felt more like wires that had been cut and had frayed. You know when you're trying to find your way somewhere and you know you're on the wrong road, and then you find the right street and it feels like an immediate relief? That's how finding this new scene felt.

Finding this group was fun and exciting—in fact, it was just as much fun as my nights in the wilder club scene, but it felt far less exploitative. For me, music is medicine. Our senses are constantly conditioning us, teaching us what to expect and what to accept, and this new scene was like a reconditioning for me. It got me calibrated to a new normal. I started a job modeling at an artist's studio. I felt really good in my body at that moment, and being surrounded by artists with an appreciation for the human form was restorative. It was the opposite of my days as a dancer. Back then, people were constantly watching me get naked, but it didn't feel natural. As an artist's model, it felt completely right. There was no perversion or sexuality to it. People were appreciating my body for the work of art that it was, and that was beautiful. Everything I did during this time was an attempt to inject culture into my life and change my consciousness, and it worked. Each small change led to another small change, until one day I looked around and the old Bea was almost gone, and a new woman had emerged. I was still cleaning, and I knew getting out of that work would be the last piece of the puzzle, but I was living with more intention, and I felt more like myself.

What's funny about consciousness is that the more aware you become, the more awareness you seek. In my early years in Atlanta, I was not searching, because I was too busy trying to get by. I was too busy partying! And even before I made it to Atlanta—when I was in Phoenix and Maryland and Phoenix again—I couldn't think bigger than the moment right in front of me, because I wasn't happy. I was focused on getting out, and not on anything deeper. And that's OK! It's all part of the journey. I have no shame or regret about any period of my life. In fact, those days of wilding out and getting my bearings taught me critical lessons that helped me get to where I am today. Making the leap from pharmacy work to cleaning and hustling gave me the courage—and the blueprint—for more important career leaps to come. And surviving those hard times required the very same skills that would eventually propel me toward success. I knew, after all that, that I could make it through anything. I knew what my version of bottom looked like, and I also knew that it was behind me.

What I didn't know in my wilder days was how to channel

my skills toward the life I wanted. Sometimes you need to live in the moment and have fun and get those urges out of your system, so that down the line you can focus on what you really want. Your twenties is the time to do it! I needed to let my hair down and lean into the life I was curious about, because if I'd resisted, that curiosity would have only gotten stronger. Still, if I wanted to find the highest version of myself, I eventually needed to find equilibrium and discover what I truly enjoyed. By the time I got my life together and settled into this new Atlanta scene, the one defined by a more intentional job and more consciousness-seeking people and a focus on health and happiness, I was existing at a higher vibration. It may seem counterintuitive, but in some ways my new life only made me hungrier. I could finally see that I was on the path to becoming who I wanted to be, but I also knew with certainty that I wasn't there yet. It was as if I could tell there was something greater out there waiting for me, and now that I wasn't distracted with the immediate urgency of *Where am I going to sleep tonight?* or *Will I be able to pay my rent?*, I couldn't ignore the bigger, maybe even harder, questions: *What am I meant for? What is my purpose?*

If I wanted to find the highest version of myself, I eventually needed to find equilibrium and discover what I truly enjoyed.

What I know now is that asking those questions, that's the first step. You can't get the answers if you aren't asking the questions. And even though I still didn't quite know where my life was going, by the time I started at Whole Foods I was in a place where I was ready to receive whatever was out there for me. In this universe, there is a method to the madness. There is a greater calling that is out there for all of us, I truly believe that. As I shifted my existence in Atlanta and focused on creating a life led with intention, I still didn't know where it was all headed. The path had begun to show itself but the destination was still shrouded in mystery. It would remain so for a little while. But sometimes all you need to know is that there *is* a destination. That's enough to keep you putting one foot in front of the other. Things might get harder before they get easier, and in many ways they did, but forward motion is like a drug. It keeps you coming back for more.

Chapter Four

There's Nothing to Be Ashamed Of

The first thing I noticed, before any discomfort, was a smell.

I'd been working at Whole Foods for about a year, and I was still focused on getting my life right. I was meeting new people, discovering new music and a new social scene, and I was also beginning to explore a new spirituality. Those were all positive developments, but I was still crazy busy—in addition to Whole Foods, I was doing the artist modeling and cleaning on the side. That's three jobs! It was a lot, and I was feeling the stress and exhaustion in my mind and my body.

Especially my body. When I'm stressed, I feel it physically. Afflictions that might be minor for others often show up big-time for me. Case in point: Not long after moving to Atlanta, I found out that I had herpes. I had an insane outbreak, one that was both so painful and so scary-looking that I went to the emergency room. I had no idea what was going on, and I was really freaked out. I remember the doctor entering my room, addressing me with this grave look in her eyes, and saying "I'm sorry to tell you, but you have herpes." Which . . . who doesn't? About one in eight American adults have genital herpes (and more than 50 percent have oral herpes), but I didn't know that at the time. Herpes is usually asymptomatic—more than 90 percent of humans who have it have no idea—and here I was having an epic outbreak. That's just how my body operates.

Some time had passed since that episode, and the herpes was pretty much under control, but one day I went to the bathroom and immediately noticed a bad, fishy odor. My period had just finished, but this was not a menstrual smell. It was different. I didn't know what was going on, and I figured it would pass, but after a few days I was not just dealing with an odor but also a lot of discharge and general discomfort. It was not pleasant, to say the least, and no matter how many showers I took or how much soap I used—and I started washing *a lot*—nothing was changing.

My doctor diagnosed me with bacterial vaginosis, or BV. I knew a bit about BV from my time working in pharmacy as well as from my work in Whole Body, where we carried products addressing vaginal infections, but now I became an expert pretty quickly. BV is an infection caused by an overgrowth of vaginal bacteria, which in turn throws a vagina's pH off balance. It's fairly common. In fact, about 35 percent of humans with vaginas will experience BV at some point in their lives, according to the Cleveland Clinic—and that percentage is even higher among Black humans with vaginas. As is the case with herpes, most people with BV never even know they have it. But I am who I am. These things hit me fully, and every possible symptom of BV appeared in my coochie like there was some sort of party in my pants.

The doctor couldn't say how or why I got BV. There are so many factors that can throw off vaginal pH—hormone levels, the wrong soap, medications, sex. It's not necessarily a sexually transmitted infection, but it's often linked to sexual activity because sex can change your pH level. Your period can throw another wrench into BV, because vaginal pH naturally rises during menstruation. Usually, it goes back to normal once your period is done, but sometimes that high pH creates a breeding ground for bacterial growth and infection.

The doctor prescribed me metronidazole, a common antibiotic for the treatment of BV. I took it as directed and the BV went away. Temporarily.

Up to 80 percent of people who get BV once will get it again, which makes sense. You may treat the infection in the moment, but if you don't change whatever daily behavior is creating a hospitable environment for the BV in the first place, it's probably going to come back. I was still washing with the same soaps. Still living with constant stress. So even though my first bout of BV went away with the meds, as soon as I got my period the next month—meaning my pH level increased once again—the BV returned. And with it, the smell and the discomfort.

My BV persisted for months. The smell would get so bad that I could stink up an entire bathroom when I pulled my pants down to pee. One time I got in a car with friends, and immediately the whole space smelled. Nobody said anything, but it was clear who had brought the odor. A car is a small space, and it was a long drive.

BV doesn't burn. It's not physically painful. But emotionally and mentally, it hurts a lot. Smelling bad, in general, is embarrassing, and when that smell is coming from your vagina—believe me, that embarrassment is even more acute. There's stigma associated with smelling bad too. Like you're dirty. "Funky vagina smell" is the kind of stupid joke men make at women's expense, despite the fact that it's both common and natural. Your vagina is not meant to smell like roses!

Intellectually, I knew that my BV was not my fault. My mom taught me from an early age that vaginas are a part of life and should not be the source of any shame. Half the population has one. She would talk to me about their power, and also their vulnerability. Genitals were not a hush-hush topic in my household, even when I was a young girl, because my mother knew that if she wasn't open with me, then if something ever happened, I might not be open with her.

She had a good reason to take this approach. My mother survived a lot of sexual trauma as a child. She was raped and molested, and as early as I can remember, she taught me about my body and about how it should be treated. "Nobody is supposed to touch you down there," she would say, "so if that ever happens, you better let me know." She drilled that into me. I'm not sure I fully understood what she was talking about or why someone would touch my vagina—I was just a kid—but I always absolutely knew that if anyone ever got handsy, I would go straight to her.

One day, when we were living in Phoenix and I was about twelve years old, my family hosted a barbecue at our home. We had a pool in our backyard—this was Arizona, it was always hot—so I was running around the house and hanging with our company wearing nothing but my bathing suit. It never occurred to me that anything was wrong with that. I was still at an age where not only was I *not* thinking about intimacy in any way, but the idea of it seemed pretty gross. Still, I was nearing my teenage years, and my body had already filled out. I had titties and curves and all the things.

That night, I went to bed, and you know that feeling where you're half asleep but you can feel something touching you? Like when you're at a sleepover with friends and they put a feather in your face so you'll swat it away in a dream state? That's basically what happened to me. I was asleep, but I kept swiping at my body because I could sense something in my space. Finally I woke up, and a member of my extended family—one who had been staying with us for a while—was lying on my bed. He was rubbing on me and touching my breasts. He hadn't made it down to my vulva yet, but he was clearly on his way. That woke me up for real, and I immediately screamed for my mother and brother. Given how many times my mom had instructed me to tell her if something like this happened, I knew she would believe me. I didn't think twice about calling for her help, and as soon as my mom and Skip showed up, I told them what my family member had done. Clearly, we couldn't have this person staying in our house anymore. That felt clear, even to my young self. Ever my protector, my mom immediately kicked him out.

Although the man in question never came into actual contact with my vulva, what I suffered was absolutely a form of sexual trauma. There was no reason for an old-ass man to be touching on me like that. To this day, I know that when I have kids, I won't let my daughter run around with just her bathing suit on past a certain age if there are men in the house. As a mama, I know I'll do whatever I think is necessary to protect my babies, just like my mommy did for me. I hate that I wouldn't let a young girl be carefree like that, but I know too much now. It's unfortunate, and it shouldn't be that way, but this abuse happens more than we know. And it has long-lasting effects. Because of this man, I was introduced to intimacy—in a completely unhealthy and nonconsensual way—at a young age, and it made me curious about sex before I should have been, or at least before I would have been otherwise. I didn't lose my virginity until I was sixteen, but I was very, very curious in the aftermath of this incident. I had a weird relationship with sex and love for a long time. I've done a lot of work to process and move past the experience, and I am grateful to be at a point where I can tell this story without feeling hurt, but I was angry for a long time.

I went through periods of questioning why I was treated this way. I'm proud that I can now recognize it as something that happened *to* me—something that absolutely should not have happened and that I wish hadn't happened—and I can see that, in its way, it made me stronger. I have also forgiven the perpetrator. I know that he's sick, because anyone who could do this to an innocent young girl is not well. I have learned that very often, the people who commit these acts have also been victims, and I have empathy for that. It's the empathy that healed me, I believe. Understanding healed me. Time healed me.

I've spoken to this family member since that interaction. It's not particularly comfortable or pleasant for me, but I have forgiven him and can have a conversation and share space with him.

Because my mother talked to me frankly about my body, both in terms of what I was entitled to (safety, privacy, respect) and the ways others might react to it, I had no shame when I was assaulted. I was disturbed and traumatized, and it was a difficult experience that I had to work hard to heal from and move past, but I didn't blame myself or my breasts or my hips or my vagina. I wasn't scared to tell my mother what had happened to me, because I was never taught—explicitly or implicitly, through a revulsion to or discomfort with words like *vagina* or *vulva*—that my feminine body was something I shouldn't talk about.

In fact, as I grew older, my mother made it a point to teach me that vaginal wellness was about more than just protecting yourself from harm. There was pleasure to be had as well. I will never forget the morning when I was fifteen and my mom took me and two friends to Denny's. The four of us were sitting at the table, eating our Grand Slams, when my mom said, "So, are you guys masturbating?" Oh man, I was so embarrassed. But she was not joking! She was just like, "You need to masturbate because you need to know what makes you feel good. You are responsible for your own pleasure. Let me tell you how I do it—I like to use my shower head." It was mortifying! But she never sugarcoated anything, because the more you talk *around* something, the more you are saying—subconsciously or not—that this thing is not something we are allowed to acknowledge out loud. So even though I couldn't believe my mother was broaching masturbation with a group of teenage girls over breakfast, now that I'm an adult I look back on that conversation with profound respect. Now, I'm like, *Damn, she was right! You* do *need to take charge of your own pleasure!*

Clearly my mom was open and honest with me, but she only told me what she felt I needed to know, when I needed to know it. She didn't throw anything at me that I couldn't handle or that I was too young to hear. As a kid, you need to know about safe touches, and what's OK and what's not. You need to know what to do if, God forbid, something scary or inappropriate happens. As humans with vaginas get older, into those teenage years of curiosity and experimentation, they need to know what they like so that they can have some agency over their own physical pleasure. It's also important to know at that age that you can get pleasure just as easily from yourself as from someone else. If there's someone in your life who isn't treating you well, giving them up doesn't mean forgoing orgasms. That's powerful knowledge.

As I got even older, my mom began enlightening me about the time in her life when she sold her body. She was honest because, first of all, this was her life and she had nothing to be ashamed of. But I think she also wanted me to understand that you do what you need to do to survive. If you ever really need something, you have a vagina. At some point in a human's life, they may have to use that vagina to get what they need. That's the message I absorbed, and it played in my head many years later when I was making the decision to go home with that couple at the Atlanta club. If I were put in the same circumstance today, I don't know that I would make the same decision, but when I was, I did what I felt I had to do. A parent can only teach a child what they know, and that's what my mom knew.

Still, despite all the work my mother put in to erase any shame around vaginal care, when I was plagued with BV month after month, I felt both self-conscious and embarrassed. I hesitated to be intimate with anyone because I didn't want to turn them off with my smell, or for them to see my abnormal amount of discharge. No matter how much I washed, I never felt clean—and if you don't feel clean, it's nearly impossible to feel confident. It was isolating and irritating, and there seemed to be no solution.

And believe me, I searched for a solution. I tried every single remedy, medical and natural, that I could find. I lived on the antibiotics for months. Eventually I dialed back to every other month because they didn't seem to be a long-term solution, and I knew from my time working in pharmacy that taking antibiotics too frequently could have the opposite effect to what I wanted. Antibiotics can change a person's microbiome, the collection of microorganisms that live in a human body. They kill off bad bacteria, which is great, but they can also kill the good ones. Taking the meds every month was actually leaving me *more* susceptible to infection because I didn't have the protection that the good bacteria provides.

I also visited an herbalist who gave me oral supplements and herbal douches to irrigate my body. They helped a bit, but not long term. I tried over-the-counter wipes and washes. I douched with water and hydrogen peroxide—a chemical that vaginas usually make naturally, and is said to protect against BV. (I know that sounds harsh, but since our bodies make their own version of hydrogen peroxide, it didn't hurt. In fact, it gave me a lot of relief, but it only worked temporarily.) I took sitz baths. (Public service announcement: Do not do this. I know now that water is more likely to mess up a recurring infection than help it.) I went on Google Forums and found anecdotal remedies that people swore by. These included putting yogurt into a tampon applicator, freezing it overnight, and inserting that inside me. It was soothing, which certainly counted for something, but it didn't heal anything. I also took a clove of garlic and wrapped it in cheesecloth and put it in my vagina like a suppository for hours at a time. Both of these remedies have ancient roots in plant-derived medicine, and they're often used to treat yeast infections as well as BV. And while they each offered me a bit of relief, they weren't *the thing*. Nothing, as far as I could tell, was *the thing*.

I went to a couple more doctors, but they all basically threw their hands up. Western medicine practitioners, in my experience, don't have training in herbal and plant medicine, and most of them don't believe in it. Their party line was clear: "These antibiotics are the only thing that can be proven to get rid of the infection." Not that doctors have always known what's best for vaginas. In the 1920s, women used to douche with Lysol in order to smell good. They also used it as a contraceptive. Advertisements in the newspaper emphatically endorsed Lysol's effectiveness as a vaginal cleanser. "She was a jewel of a wife . . . with just one flaw," explains one such ad. "She was guilty of the 'one neglect' that mars many marriages. Lysol helps avoid this."

Another ad read: "Day after heartbreaking day I was held in an unsuspecting web . . . a web spun by my husband's indifference. I couldn't reach him anymore! Was the fault mine? Well . . . thinking you know about feminine hygiene, yet trusting to *now-and-then* care, can make all the difference in married happiness, as my doctor pointed out. He said never to run such careless risks . . . prescribed Lysol-brand disinfectant for douching—always."

There is so much wrong with this ad: The emphasis on douching for marital happiness, for one. And the idea that a doctor recommended a cleaner, one meant to disinfect toilets or dirty kitchens, *for the vagina*. And, of course, the idea that the smell of your vagina is something to be blamed for or ashamed of. This messaging was sold to all women, but Black women especially, due to long-held racist narratives around their "smelliness" or "dirtiness." And Lysol back then had an even more dangerous chemical makeup than it does today—it included a compound called cresol, which was reported to cause vaginal inflammation and burning, and in a few cases even death. By the 1940s, using Lysol as a douche reportedly became the most popular form of birth control in the country (though not an effective one—one study found that about half the women who used it ended up getting pregnant). In 1952, Lysol changed its formula to be a bit less toxic, but it still was not safe for vaginas, causing blistering and bleeding for some women. It was completely wrecking women's systems. It's crazy to think of this now, but the reality is that Lysol as a douche only waned in popularity once the birth control pill came around in the 1960s.

No one was suggesting at this point that I disinfect my vagina, but I still knew that Western medicine doctors didn't necessarily have all the answers. I wasn't insisting on an herbal treatment, but I'd already given the antibiotics their fair shake, and I still smelled. Part of the roadblock with my doctors, I began to realize, was that they were focused on treatment. When the problem popped up, they wanted to fix it. But I knew by then that just treating the current issue wasn't going to be enough. I wanted to do something proactive. I needed to prevent it from coming back.

The human body is all one system. If your pH is off, if you're stressed, if you're anxious, if you're depressed, if you're using the wrong soap or the wrong skincare—any one of those imbalances can throw off the entire system. I understood that interconnectedness from my years working in pharmacy. I also knew that an infection, while not something any of us *wants*, is essentially your body's way of communicating to you that something is wrong. *Our system is out of balance, and we need to recalibrate.* Of course we see this as a nuisance, but it could also be reframed as a gift: Your body is willing to show you that something unusual or unhelpful is going on. Still, it's hard to keep that perspective when it feels like your body is betraying you.

Because I knew that recurring infections were a sign of imbalance, I started second-guessing everything. One major issue was that the bar soap I was using was not balanced for my vulva and my vagina, which was only worsening the situation. But my re-examination extended across all areas of my life. *What was I doing wrong? Why was this happening to me?*

One thing I knew for certain was that I was under an unusual amount of stress. I was working multiple jobs, and still scrambling to make ends meet. I had recently entered into a long-distance romance with a man who lived in London, and the relationship was not a healthy one. It would be a long time until I came to openly acknowledge or accept how bad things were, but when you're in a relationship that's wrong for you—even if you only know it subconsciously—you often find yourself feeling more lonely than if you were actually alone. My life was difficult in nearly every aspect, so maybe it was no wonder that my body was out of whack. But none of my problems had easy answers.

This struggle went on for eight months. Eight months of discomfort. Eight months of embarrassment and shame. Eight months of false hope, thinking I'd gotten my body under control, only to be disappointed about twenty-eight days later. It was like *Groundhog Day*, every day running into the same brick wall, every day questioning my ability to take care of myself.

During these same eight months, there were a couple of positives in my life. My mother had left Arizona and moved to Atlanta to live closer to me. We moved in together and were roommates again after being apart for years. I'd also begun to discover the spirituality that would become a huge part of my life. About a year earlier, a friend had told me she was going to get a "reading," and it sparked my curiosity.

"What's a reading?" I asked.

"It's basically a religious ceremony," she said. "You sit at the feet of a priest and get insight into where you are in your life now, and where you should go in the future."

Until then, I had never really connected to a religion. As a kid, our family practiced Christianity, though we weren't particularly devout. It was more of a "do what you know" situation, and since my mom's family practiced Christianity, so did we. In reality, my mom was more spiritual than she was religious, though we didn't really have an understanding of the difference back then. She was always tapped into the God inside of her. She didn't force religion on us, but my siblings and I went to church from time to time. Certainly not every Sunday. I went to Bible study occasionally too, but it was hard for me to connect to the religion or the culture that was associated with it. I was in the church choir for a minute, for example, but I didn't especially enjoy gospel music. Some people absolutely love it, but I just didn't feel it deeply the way others around me did. I remember going on church trips—teen retreats, basically—and let me tell you, we were not behaving like good Christian children! I got baptized when I was about sixteen, but as I got older and developed a stronger sense of self, my soul and my spirit just didn't feel settled in this religion. The idea that not believing, or not being baptized, meant you would go to hell was always very hard for me. If you didn't accept Jesus Christ as your Lord and Savior, then you wouldn't be saved, and that brought up many more questions for me than it answered. What happened with Hindus and Muslims and people that practiced other spiritualties? What about Buddhist monks and nuns? They meditate all day! They can't all be going to hell.

My life was difficult in nearly every aspect, so maybe it was no wonder that my body was out of whack. But none of my problems had easy answers.

Religion and spirituality are very personal, and I'm not saying that anyone who believes in the teachings of Christianity, or of any belief system, is wrong. If you follow the teachings of Jesus or Buddha or Elijah Muhammad, that's your choice—it's the beauty of the world we live in. You can believe in the Devil if you want; I'm not here to tell anybody what is right or wrong. But in my personal journey, questions plagued me that caused me to distance myself from the religion of my childhood.

As I think back on it today, I can see that much of my evolution had nothing to do with Christianity and everything to do with me. By the time I was in my late twenties, I was ready for a new school of thought. There is something so interesting to me about the fact that we have different schools for tapping into God. There's something really beautiful about it. I'm not sure I was cognizant of this back then, but I know now that I had gotten what I needed from Christianity, and my spirit wanted more. I was in a period of searching—I was looking for my professional calling and for meaningful and productive relationships and, yes, a new relationship to God and religion. I was tapped into the fact that there was a source, but I was having trouble connecting to it. I used to listen to the song "Searching" by Roy Ayers on repeat. It really made me feel seen, because I was looking for myself almost desperately at that point.

My friend's reading sounded like something that would help me, so I tagged along with her. I met with a Yoruba priest, and even in that first session I was overwhelmed by how powerful it was—this man knew things about me that he had no logical way of knowing. It piqued my interest, and I immediately began to learn more.

Yoruba is a West African spiritual practice and tradition. One that has heavily influenced religions including Santeria, which developed in Cuba; Candomblé, which developed in Brazil; and Orisha in Trinidad. During the slave trade, Africans who were forced from their homes brought their own religions with them, and over time those beliefs evolved into different religions in different locations. Santeria developed among Afro-Cubans, though it is increasingly popular in the U.S. these days. It's a beautiful belief system—one that reveres and pays respect to the gods of the ocean and the sky and lightning and wind. It celebrates and worships the gods of nature. It's also heavily focused on ancestry—you have to pay respect to those who came before you. There is a lot of Native in my blood, and there are a lot of similarities between Santeria and Native culture—honoring nature and ancestors especially—which contributed to how deeply Santeria appealed to me.

Getting initiated into Santeria is no small undertaking. The initiation ceremony took place in Cuba—it was a hard-core ceremony, the intricacies of which had to be kept private (and still do) for only those who were present—but it immersed me in religion in a way I'd never experienced. For the next year, I had to wear only white. I had to shave off all my hair. I wasn't allowed to look in mirrors. When I say it was life-changing, I don't mean it in the typical "it was amazing!" way. I mean it literally changed my fucking life, in nearly every single way.

Because Santeria is defined in large part by its emphasis on our lineage, my initiation ceremony involved invoking my ancestors more deliberately than I ever had in the past. I got more intentional about creating a clear and open path between me and those who came before me. I was constantly saying their names and lighting a candle to let them know that I loved them and appreciated them.

My mother, now also my roommate, wasn't completely comfortable with my religious evolution. She was a Christian, and what I was practicing was totally new to her. But she's also my mom, and she knows me better than anyone. When she moved to Atlanta, she could see that I was going through it. I was suffering, physically, from BV. I was exhausted, mentally, from working multiple jobs. I was in a romantic relationship that caused me emotional turmoil. My mother witnessed all of this, so no matter how skeptical she was of my new religion, she also saw that my commitment to the spirituality was improving my well-being. My life, in general, was taking a more purposeful turn. It was finally organized. I don't mean that in the literal sense of putting stuff in boxes, although on an emotional level that *is* what I was doing. Not compartmentalizing exactly, which I'd define as denying certain emotions or burying parts of yourself so you can succeed in others. But *organizing*. I was beginning to understand what I was feeling in any given moment, and why. I was establishing a better sense of how to deal with or accept my feelings as they came up. It's not that I was suddenly happy all the time—clearly I was not—but I wasn't beating myself up for my feelings and or denying them, either. I was noticing my emotions and accepting them as they appeared. My mom knew this was good for me, so she accepted my religious choice.

When I returned from the initiation trip to Cuba, my spirit was as open as it had ever been. That one area of my life was beautiful and abundant. Nothing is ever all easy or all hard, all good or all bad, and there's usually a reason for that. One side feeds the other, as I was about to find out.

*

I have always been a vivid dreamer. I usually do my heaviest dreaming in the morning, right before I wake up. One day, not long after I returned home from Cuba, I had an early morning dream in which I was sitting in white clothes, in a white room, surrounded by white light. There was a white tablecloth and white chairs. It was an inviting and peaceful and truly beautiful space. I sat in that room opposite a woman who was also dressed in white. I didn't know who she was exactly, but I knew she was a close relation. I'd never seen her before, but she looked like me. The women on my mom's side have strong facial features. We all look alike, so I could tell she came from that lineage. I was excited and honored to have a visit from an ancestor I didn't know, and I tried to say as much. Although, when I talk to my ancestors, it's not the way I might talk to a person on the street. We don't use audible words; it's more telepathic. It's them making me understand something, or showing me something. We share messages mentally because this is a spiritual communication. It doesn't need to be spoken out loud.

So, in our way, in the dream, I shared with this woman how nice it was to see her and meet her. She shut me down real quick.

"I'm not here for that," she said, in our telepathic way. "I can't stay long and we've got things to do, so let's get to it." She explained to me that she'd been walking with me, and she'd seen me struggling. She knew what I needed to do.

"OK, I see you," I said. "I hear you."

She handed me a piece of paper with a list of ingredients and pointed at it. I recited the ingredients, and she signaled to me to repeat myself. I said the ingredients a second time.

Again, she signaled. Again. Again.

I must have repeated those ingredients a hundred times, over and over, and she just kept signaling me to run them again, until suddenly she screamed, "Wake up!!!!"

Now that part I heard. It was not telepathic. She was pushing me into the conscious world.

My eyes popped open and I immediately shot upright. It was like in the movies, when a character wakes up and realizes she missed her alarm. I was sitting up in my bed, reciting the ingredients before I even realized what was happening.

Coconut oil, apple cider vinegar, rose, lavender, garlic, grapefruit seed extract.

Coconut oil, apple cider vinegar, rose, lavender, garlic, grapefruit seed extract.

Coconut oil, apple cider vinegar, rose, lavender, garlic, grapefruit seed extract.

I was reciting this list on repeat, over and over, and quickly grabbed a piece of paper and wrote the ingredients down before I could lose them. My mom was in the next room, so I rushed to tell her what happened.

"Holy shit, I just met one of my ancestors and she told me a list of ingredients. I think she wants me to make a product," I said.

I explained to my mom what this woman looked like. I told her about the white light and the shared facial features.

My mom looked at me as though the explanation was obvious. "That was your grandmother."

Later that day, I reported to my shift at Whole Foods, and while I was there, I bought all the ingredients on my list.

When I got back home, my spidey senses were up. I could tell even before I got to work that something big was happening. I was onto something. I knew that the ingredients my grandmother shared made sense. Vinegar helps balance pH and neutralize odor; lavender is calming and antimicrobial; coconut oil cleans and adds a soap texture; rose water is hydrating and cooling. One of the messages my grandmother had shared with me in the dream was that I was already using a lot of the right ingredients, like the garlic, but those ingredients needed to come together in the right way to make a potion.

I stood in my kitchen, staring at the ingredients I had laid out on the counter. *Where do I start?* My grandmother had told me what to get, but she didn't give me a formula or any sort of instructions. She knew I could formulate because I had experience in pharmaceutical work. I'm not a chemist, but I'd seen enough to learn a thing or two, and I spent some time that evening researching online how to make a skincare product. It was only a baseline refresher, but enough to make me think, *OK, Bea. You got this.* I'd bought a couple of extra products at work that day—sandalwood, hydrogen peroxide—because I thought they would help, and I just started experimenting. A lot of skincare products, lotions, and oils are batched and made with heat, but what I was making wasn't a warm formulation. I was creating something cool, which meant I just needed to put in the right ingredients at the right time in the right ratio and mix the right amount. I'd purchased a lot of each ingredient, since I didn't know how much I'd need or how many tries it would take, so I stood in my kitchen with a giant mixing bowl and, like a witch with her cauldron, just started iterating. By the end of the night, I had created a version of a wash and put it in an old salsa bottle to keep in my shower.

I had no idea if what I'd made would work. How could I? But I knew that it probably couldn't hurt. The worst-case scenario, I figured, was that it would do nothing, and then I'd be back to square one. I'd been at square one for eight months. I was permanently stuck at square fucking one. At this point, all I could do was try.

I washed myself religiously with the potion I'd made. Twice a day every day for a week. Within five days, I noticed that the smell was gone. I cannot overstate how powerful that was. It almost immediately calmed me down. To shudder at your own scent is an incredibly shameful feeling. It also keeps you fixated on a problem. Scent is in many ways our most powerful sense. It may not be considered the most "important," but it can cause visceral reactions. An especially bad smell, for example, can make a person gag. A good smell can trigger fond memories and emotions. *Not* noticing my own smell meant that, at least for a few days, I just didn't think about my vagina. That alone felt like freedom! I wasn't fixated on what was wrong with me. I wasn't wracking my brain trying to come up with another possible solution. I had spent the last eight months worried almost every single day, and now this heavy burden had been lifted off me, if only for a moment.

The fact that this solution came from an ancestor—it was very comforting for me. There's something so healing about getting a message from the beyond. When a spirit comes to you and tells you to do something, that in itself is a gift, because you finally know what action to take and you can trust in that knowing. I hope it goes without saying that I'm not talking about a directive to do something harmful—you can't rob a bank or commit violence and chalk it up to "the spirits told me to"—but for me, in this particular instance, I knew my grandmother was looking out for me. I knew she was protecting me, and that care, it was like magic. It was no coincidence that my grandmother came when she did. I'd been vigilantly attending to my ancestors through my spirituality, even in the midst of my own physical and emotional turmoil. The door for those who wanted to visit from beyond was sitting ajar, welcoming people through. I'd created the perfect environment for my grandmother to say, *Let me go help my baby, because she don't know what she's doing.*

She gifted me with healing.

Less than a week after I started using the wash, everything changed. My smell subsided completely. My panties were not covered in discharge. Nothing, not even the antibiotics, had worked this quickly and this well, and—even more incredible—the next month, it didn't come back. For a couple months, I simply enjoyed the freedom of *not* thinking about my vagina every second of every day. But soon after that, the magnitude of what had happened hit me. I'd created something that solved a problem! My formula worked! At this point, there were no companies out there talking about the vaginal issues that I'd been grappling with for months. No one was speaking openly and honestly about vaginal health. Instead, all the companies who tried to occupy the "feminine wellness" space coded their language in euphemisms. I'd been searching for information about vaginal health that promoted self-love rather than embarrassment, and it just didn't exist.

No one was speaking openly and honestly about vaginal health. Instead, all the companies who tried to occupy the "feminine wellness" space coded their language in euphemisms.

Our bodies are our temples. They are beautiful and amazing no matter what your vagina smells like or what you weigh or what color your skin. Going through BV made me lose sight of that. I was too ashamed and embarrassed to really love myself. Taking charge of my healing helped me reclaim power over my own body, and, I finally realized, it gave me a new purpose.

I will never forget the moment, sitting on the toilet, when it occurred to me that I hadn't emitted a horrendous odor in days.

It suddenly hit me: *This is what I do now.*

Chapter Five

If You Don't Think Big, Nobody Will

I did not make my first wash with any ulterior motive other than to heal myself. I didn't even know if I'd achieve that, but at the time I started formulating, my own health and physical relief was all I could think about. When you're in pain, it's hard to expand your thinking beyond yourself. But professionally, I still hadn't let go of the dream that maybe one day I could own my schedule. That I could report to only myself. I didn't enjoy cleaning houses, but it gave me a taste of entrepreneurship. I set my own hours and landed my own clients and I was responsible for how I made and spent money. Even when I danced at the strip club it felt like a form of entrepreneurship, because I was using my body to get what I wanted and what I needed. Or trying to, anyhow. It wasn't the most abundant side of entrepreneurship for me personally, but it taught me what it was like to be out in the world and eat what you kill. I never finished college, and I wouldn't have been interested in going to business school in the traditional sense, but I went to the hard-knocks version. And as it turned out, I liked it. I certainly didn't enjoy just barely scraping by and always playing catch-up, but I appreciated the autonomy that working for myself afforded.

One thing I've always known inherently is that all we have is time—that is a human's only real currency. Everything else is made up. So when I got a taste of owning mine, it was hard to give that up. I didn't want to punch a clock, and I wasn't very good at it. Even at Whole Foods, I was one of the top salespeople on the floor, but I clocked in late every single day. My boss, Nina, whom I'm still friends with to this day, would look at me when I arrived each morning like, *Girl. Come on.* And I was doing my best, but it was my time! Not theirs!

One of things I enjoyed most when I was working at Whole Foods was meeting with the different companies and brands and brokers behind the products we sold. Whenever I had a chance to connect with the people behind these businesses, I felt a yearning inside me, like, *This is what I'm supposed to be doing.* I've always been a healer. Creating a wellness brand or product, it felt like it made sense for me, and yet I couldn't quite figure out what to do with that sensation. You know when you're trying to light a match, and you strike it and strike it and the spark is there but the flame doesn't quite catch? Every meeting with a brand felt like that for me. Like something was there, but I wasn't sure what. So when I realized that this concoction I created actually *worked*? It was like that match finally lit up. It hit me that if this worked for me, it could work for other people.

Pretty quickly, my kitchen started to double as a laboratory. I experimented with bottling, adding new herbs, adjusting the product's texture, and tweaking the fragrance. I asked Simon to come help me. Simon came to Atlanta from Boston by way of London and Jamaica, and he's had to bust his ass for everything he has. He put himself through school, graduated, worked in finance, and then left the company he worked for to start his own accounting firm. This was a man who was not only brilliant but who knew how to pull himself up by his bootstraps, and I knew he respected that kind of drive in other people. We just always rode for each other, so when I told him what I was working on and he realized I was going to need funds to keep buying ingredients and bottles and the like, he agreed to partner with me. He gave me a credit card with a $500 balance.

> One thing I've always known inherently is that all we have is time—that is a human's only real currency. Everything else is made up. So when I got a taste of owning mine, it was hard to give that up.

Some trials went better than others. Occasionally, the result was just gross. But the core ingredients that my grandmother gifted me never really changed. And while I felt confident that we were onto something, Simon and I knew then what we know now: Every body is different. Just because this wash helped me didn't necessarily mean it would do the same for other people. We had to do the research and the testing that would allow us to stand behind the product.

Luckily, I worked in the exact right place. In the Whole Body department, we had plenty of customers who were looking for natural remedies for vaginal issues. Even before I made my first wash, whenever a customer came in with a vaginal concern, my team would send her my way. There were only six of us working in our department. We had become friends, and everyone who knew me at that time knew that I was struggling with recurring BV, because I was on a very determined journey to fix myself. Anytime a customer came in with a similar ailment, it was "go talk to Bea," because I'd tried everything. I would show them the probiotics and the herbs that help with dryness and the natural suppositories for a yeast issue and help them figure out what made the best sense for them. Once I had my own product, I would do the same thing, but then I would walk them to the register and offer to help them to their car. When we were out

> We have always been driven by our dedication to people's bodies and our insistence that we are responsible about what we're making.

of the building, I would tell them about my journey and offer to give them a sample of my product for free. All I asked for in return was feedback. Some customers thought it was a little weird, but most of the time, when your coochie is messed up, you'll try anything. Most of the people shopping for vaginal remedies happily accepted what I was offering because they wanted whatever help they could get.

Simon and I proceeded this way for two years: working on the wash, giving it away, gathering feedback. Honey Pot has been a test-and-learn type of company since before we were even really a company. Since before we had the name Honey Pot! Back then, we were calling it "The Happy Root." Obviously a lot has changed, but a lot has stayed the same: We have always been driven by our dedication to people's bodies and our insistence that we are responsible about what we're making. Over the course of those couple years, we probably gave away at least a hundred free bottles of wash, with eight out of ten customers claiming positive results. They'd tell me what a relief it was to wear silk panties again without fear of ruining them with discharge, or to no longer have mysterious odors emanating from their workout pants after going to the gym. We weren't technically in clinical trials back then, but this feedback felt just as valuable. Eventually, repeat customers felt bad taking my product for free, so they began to pay whatever they felt was right.

That small influx of cash was welcomed, because my grandmother's ingredients were not cheap. It honestly felt like a sign from the universe that I'd had enough money to afford the first batch of groceries on the morning I received her visit. But to continue to make the wash in larger quantities, we were going to need more financial help. We would also need a larger audience. We needed to expand beyond the customers who happened to wander into Whole Foods looking to fix their vaginas.

Atlanta, it turns out, is home to one of the largest beauty trade shows in the world, the Bronner Bros. International Beauty Show. Known more casually as the Bronner Bros. Hair Show, it's held twice a year and is one of the biggest conventions in the Black beauty industry. As soon as I learned about this show, I knew that getting a booth would be the perfect opportunity to put the product in front of a wider audience. But it wouldn't be cheap. Sy is a numbers guy, and he knew that a booth at a high-profile event like the Hair Show would run our costs up significantly. He wasn't convinced it was the best move. After all, he had his own stuff going on, including a thriving company. He didn't need to invest energy or funds into a start-up that was not yet even selling product. He wasn't totally sure what the future of this company looked like. I couldn't be sure either, but I really thought this was our chance, and I wasn't too proud to beg. The day I told him about the show, I literally got down on hands and knees. "Please, Sy, help us find the money to do this," I said. "If it doesn't work, I will *never* ask you for another penny. Never! But I really think it's going to work."

Eventually I wore him down. "OK, let's do it," Sy said. He pulled in another close friend, Troy, who had just come into some money, and together they funneled $20,000 into the business. It was incredibly generous, and I was so grateful. I had never seen that much money in one place. We used it to pay for a well-designed booth and banner for the Hair Show, bottles and caps, and the ingredients to account for hundreds of bottles of product. In all my life—even when I was flat broke and struggling to find a place to stay or food to eat—I had never asked anyone to borrow that kind of money. I might have asked to crash on a couch, but never did I make a request for straight cash. Still, this felt different. I wasn't looking for a handout just to get me through to my next paycheck. I was looking for an investment, because I believed with my whole heart and soul that this product could be big. I was very clear with Simon: "If this doesn't work, I will not bring it up to you again as long as we live. But if it does, it could change our lives."

Around this same time, I was driving home from work one day, and while stopped at a red light, I noticed a telephone pole with a flyer for a band called the Honey Pot. I loved the name, and I knew the phrase was an old colloquialism for vagina. Suddenly, I had everything I needed: a partnership with Simon, access to the funds we needed to go to the Hair Show, and the idea for a proper business name, The Honey Pot Company.

To prepare for the Hair Show, Simon and I recruited friends and family and put together an assembly line in his office. This group was responsible for bottling the product that I was now calling "the normal wash." After two years of tinkering, the ingredients hadn't changed much. The normal wash was a foaming blend of water, saponified coconut oil soap, rosewater, lavender water, grapefruit seed extract, garlic extract, and apple cider vinegar. We got six hundred bottles of product ready for the show, but it wasn't just wash we needed to prepare. We also needed a booth, one that would attract customers who came to this convention center to check out hair products, not vagina products. I had never designed a booth, but I knew the space had to be cute and that people needed to be visually drawn to it. This was a massive convention center—the big leagues!—and we were going to be competing for attention with companies that had money, which meant their spaces would be heavily designed and eye-catching. We didn't have the cash flow for all that, so instead we decided to put all the natural ingredients on display and really showcase the plant-derived elements that set us apart. We had apples, coconuts, and lavender all over our table, and it definitely had a different vibe than the booths around us. It felt calming, almost Zen, especially in a room full of hair products that sometimes relied on toxic chemicals to get their intended results.

The Hair Show was three days long—Friday, Saturday, and Sunday. Simon and I were working the Honey Pot booth along with Suad, Simon's cousin; my mother; and our friends Indra, Justin, and Dom. We paid them all to help out, but we didn't have much, so they didn't make any meaningful money from it. They were just there out of the goodness of their hearts.

The first few hours of that Friday were rough. It was hard to get people to stop at our booth, and those that did were skeptical of why they'd need a vagina wash. When our first customers wandered up to our booth, instead of going into any kind of clever pitch—because I hadn't had any time to come up with one—I just shared my story. I explained that I had BV and wasn't able to get rid of it for months until my grandma came to me in a dream. I shared that I was able to heal myself, which made me want to offer the wash to others who might be suffering. People loved the story, but they also didn't see what it had to do with them.

"I don't have BV," they'd say. After all, these weren't Whole Foods customers I'd cornered because I knew their coochie was in trouble. These were people looking for hair care! I'd explain that the product wasn't just for people with BV, it was for people with vaginas. It was a wash for your vulva that could help you prevent any issues before they even arise. Some people listened, some people laughed, but a bigger problem than these reactions was that we just weren't getting the foot traffic we needed at our booth. By midday Friday we changed course, and rather than waiting for people to come to us, we went to them. The friends and family who had helped us formulate and bottle the product were now mingling with the crowd, some handing out flyers, others carrying our wash in a foaming pump dispenser and offering to let people try it on their hands. The one thing we had working in our favor was that this was a convention center full of people with vaginas. Our clientele was all around us; we just had to get through to them.

Once enough people in the crowd had had a sensory experience with our wash—the unassuming scent, the calming texture even just on their hands—they started to get more curious. By Friday afternoon, we had found our groove. Our booth had a steady stream of potential customers. And if Friday was busy, Saturday was hammer time. It was the weekend, so already the show was busier than it had been the day before. Plus, plenty of people had gone home the previous night and tried the wash, and now they were back for more. For three days straight, we were on our feet from 9 a.m. to 6 p.m., just selling, selling, and more selling. It was exhausting, but also exhilarating. I needed this to work, because if it didn't, I'd promised Sy that I would never bring it up again. I gave it all I had, but so did our whole team.

By the end of the day on Sunday, we'd sold every last bottle of wash. If we hadn't been sure whether Honey Pot had a future, now we had our answer.

Now that we had tangible proof that this company appealed to people and could really be something, I allowed myself to dream big. We started by making it official, or as official as you can be when you're flying by the seat of your pants: I would be the Honey Pot CEO and Simon would be our CFO. We didn't have a contract, but we had each other and that's what mattered to us.

I wrote myself a check for a million dollars and pasted it to my ceiling. It was the first thing I saw when I woke up in the morning and the last thing I saw before I went to sleep at night. That check symbolized everything I was working for, and it helped me set the intention that Honey Pot would make its first million just by me and Simon and our soon-to-be-team doing its best. If I ever forgot why I was working so hard, there it was: six zeroes staring me in the face. Of course, Honey Pot was never just about making money, but it *was* a business, and businesses need to profit to survive.

Writing that check wasn't simply a matter of wishful thinking. I wasn't trying to be cute. It was a physical representation of what I was now absolutely certain was going to happen eventually.

After the show we launched a website, and I could feel the forward momentum of this business. We started growing our team. We met a woman named Linda at our second Hair Show, and she was a big fan of the product and offered to help us grow. She ultimately became our first CMO. About a year later, we brought in a woman named Antoinee, who was basically my right hand—she helped make and bottle product in my kitchen, and helped with packaging and mailing. Eventually we hired other integral team members, like Kelly, who worked in sales, and Suad, who helped with our trade shows. It was a team effort, and the more our group grew, the more legit our business felt. Plus, it was a pleasure to be surrounded by other people who were dedicated to the same end goal and believed in this company and wanted to make it great. I felt very lucky.

And yet, I still needed to make a living. Every dollar that we made off Honey Pot went back into Honey Pot. That's the reality when you are trying to build and grow a business, which meant I needed to get some money into my own pocket. I loved my job at Whole Foods, but soon I got offered an opportunity to work as a food broker. I'd worked with brokers from this company when I worked at Whole Foods, and I was ready for something new, that paid a little bit better, and that afforded me more freedom since I'd be working on my own, traveling to different stores.

I represented about a hundred brands, and my job was to go into three stores a day and try to sell the buyers on whatever brands I was pushing, so that they would in turn sell the products in their stores. Often that meant giving them the first case of the product for free. "Once you sell out, all you have to do is order more," I'd explain. As a broker, I took the same approach to getting Honey Pot in stores as I did to giving it away to customers in my Whole Foods days. I would go into the little grocery stores in my territory as Bea Dixon, food broker, and sell them whatever I was there to sell them. Then I would walk out of the store and walk back in as Bea Dixon, Honey Pot founder, and sell them the wash. I only had a couple of minutes because I didn't have my own appointment with the buyer—I was using my relationship with them to borrow a moment of their time. I'd quickly tell them the whole backstory of the product, and explain that they didn't have anything on their shelves that was solving this problem for their customers. I knew this was true, because I'd spent time in their stores. "I'm going to give you three to six bottles of the wash, complimentary," I'd say. "When I come back next month, if they haven't sold, I'll take them off your hands and you never have to talk to me about it again. But if they have, you can buy it from me directly."

It seemed like a no-brainer to me, but not everyone jumped at the offer. I thought I'd have a harder time with men, but the truth is everyone was hesitant, no matter their gender. I was working with a lot of natural food stores, and in that world, vaginal brands weren't always embraced. The party line in the natural wellness world was that "the vagina is a self-cleaning oven," so products like washes and wipes were taboo. While that statement has some truth to it, the vagina is inside the body. I was selling products for the vulva—the external genitalia. It was vaginal wellness, but the product itself did not go in the vagina. I was constantly running into that brick wall, but my answer to the skeptics was always the same: Just offer it. There's no way these people used or believed in every product in their store. They had tons of products on their shelves that they probably wouldn't use, but they carried them because their customers liked them. "You may not need it or want it," I'd say, "but you can't choose for your customers, and this is a product that is all natural. If that's the requirement to be on your shelves, then we belong here." That was my go-to rebuttal, and it worked a lot of the time. No matter what a buyer's reason was to resist—they weren't all the same—I always had a counterpoint. In sales, you need to have your rebuttal ready, because there are always going to be nos. Your job is to get to a yes.

My sales strategy for Honey Pot was a grassroots one. And since I had connections and a history at my local Whole Foods,

I was able to get the product in there, too. It was just one store, and they didn't order it in the numbers I hoped they would, or for the price I hoped they'd pay—we basically gave it to them for free; in fact, it probably *cost* us money—but that didn't matter. We knew the value of being in Whole Foods, and of being able to *say* we were in Whole Foods. It was another notch in our belt that would open other doors.

Building a business looks intimidating and scary from the outside, but the reality is that if you take it one step at a time, you can find yourself looking up and thinking, *Wait a minute, when did this happen?* That's how it felt for us at Honey Pot. Not that the company happened overnight, because it absolutely didn't. We worked hard! In fact, I think it's what I was training for my whole life. All that hustling and cleaning and dancing and modeling, it was my own version of boot camp, preparing me for this professional battle. Because starting a business while you are also working full-time is *a lot*. It is not for the faint of heart. Plenty of people do it, and I had no other choice than to keep working my day job because I needed money to live, and I

I was propelled by my sheer desire to make this company into something. I don't know that I have ever wanted anything or believed in anything as much as I wanted and believed in Honey Pot. I wanted to build something of my own. I wanted to serve humanity.

couldn't take food out of Honey Pot's mouth. It was like an infant. It needed everything! And also, I had no idea what I was doing. I didn't have any training in starting or growing a business. It certainly helped to have Simon as a cofounder, since he went to school for finance. He had book smarts and accounting experience. He taught me so much. But even if you go to business school and get all the "necessary training," it doesn't mean your idea is going to take off or your company is going to hit. Luckily, we had more than just good training. Simon and I were a good partnership because he had the know-how and I had the hunger. I was propelled by my sheer desire to make this company into something. I don't know that I have ever wanted anything or believed in anything as much as I wanted and believed in Honey Pot. I wanted to build something of my own. I wanted to serve humanity. Today, people ask me all the time "Did you ever think Honey Pot could be this big?" and I give them the honest answer: Hell motherfucking yeah! When I believe in something, I only know how to think big. I couldn't have predicted our exact path, and at the beginning I couldn't even articulate exactly what I wanted for this company. But I have never doubted myself when it comes to my drive and hustle, and when you have those things you can figure out the rest. I knew Honey Pot could be something bigger than it was, as long as I kept working.

It took two years for Honey Pot to go from a single bottle in my kitchen to six hundred bottles at the Hair Show, and then another year for it to land on a shelf in Whole Foods. But once it did? Well, that was major. It didn't matter that we were only in one store; we were officially carried at Whole Foods, which lent us credibility. I felt like we were on the cusp of something, if only we could put a little more cash into the business.

"I think we need to raise more money," I told Simon one day.

"It's not time," Simon said. "You'll know when it's time."

I didn't know what he was talking about, but I knew I needed Simon's buy-in, because he was the one who knew how to fund-raise. He was the one with the Rolodex of high-net-worth individuals, because that's who uses CPAs, and those would be the first people we'd approach for money when the time was right. And, he was my business partner. We'd been working together since pretty much the beginning, and I trusted his instincts and respected his input.

Every time we got into a new store or saw a bunch of orders on the website, I'd say it again, "I think we need to raise more money." We were still using my kitchen as our manufacturing facility. Every day, the table was covered in five-gallon containers—the kind with a spigot that you'd usually use for tea or lemonade—as well as beakers, measuring cups, mixing spoons, measuring spoons, mixing sticks, and of course the ingredients for the wash. At this point it was mostly me and Antoinee in my kitchen. One of us was always holding a paper and pen, calculating the ingredient proportions or the number of bottles we needed for the current batch. We had gotten the formulation down to a science. First, we would pour water into the big container, then we'd add the first batch of ingredients and mix it one hundred times. Not ninety-nine, not one hundred and one. Then we'd add the next set of ingredients and mix that. The last step would be to add the essential oils and herbs. After mixing it all in the five-gallon containers, we would clean up the beakers and mixers and replace them with an assembly line for the bottles. Before we could put any product in the bottles we had to wash them and the caps. Next, we filled the bottles one by one, capped them all off, and put them each in a shrink sleeve. A shrink sleeve is the label that wraps around a bottle, and it has to be applied with heat—that's what makes the label tighten around the container—so we would manually blow them with a hair dryer. We literally stood there with a hair dryer pointed at hundreds of bottles. On the evenings when we had the energy, we'd wipe everything down, put it all away, and turn the room back into a kitchen. But more often, at that point, we would just eat out or order in.

We were also going to more festivals and trade shows, which obviously cost money, and I had ideas for ways to expand beyond washes, because I'd realized that a wash alone couldn't maintain a growing business. Even if a wash works wonders, people are only going to come back for more every six to eight weeks. But one thing I understood intuitively was that a single vagina will go through so many issues over the course of a lifetime. As a young girl, a human with a vagina might be getting baths with baby products that are formulated for young skin, but not for little vulvas. Or she may not have been taught how to wipe properly, and so she's getting UTIs or yeast infections as a result. That's the same human who will grow up and get her period and need pads or tampons, and the same human who will grow up some more and start having sex and need lube. That sexually active human might get bacterial vaginosis and need a wash, and she might get pregnant and deliver a baby and need post-partum vaginal care or support for incontinence. She will eventually go through perimenopause and then menopause. It occurred to me early in Honey Pot's life that there was an opportunity for us serve that vagina through all of these phases, and no one else was doing that. The state of vaginal wellness even as recently as 2014 was almost entirely rooted in shame—when you used a wash it was to cover up an odor, not to fix a pH balance for wellness. Vaginal wellness was simply not a thing. There were conglomerates in the menstrual space, and others in the hygiene space, but no feminine hygiene brand had ever crossed the aisle into menstrual, and no menstrual brand had ever gotten into washes or wipes or douches. No company had taken on vaginal wellness holistically, where they told the story all the way through, and I saw an opportunity there. I'm not sure why no one else ever did. I don't know what is in anyone else's head, but I believe I was aided by the fact that I take humans with vaginas very seriously.

Unfortunately, there was no way we could try to create more products with just the cash we were making—it was barely enough to keep the operation running. There was no extra for experimentation. Instead, Linda and I came up with the idea to sell other companies' products on our site. Through my work as a food broker, I had access to other brands, so in 2015 we brought in a company that made wipes and another company that made pads and another company that made mommy and baby products and we started selling them on our website. We wanted to understand what else our customers wanted from us, and this allowed us to conduct that research without spending money on creating our own product.

Once we started selling a wider range of vaginal wellness products, Honey Pot grew from doing $30,000 a year to $240,000 a year in sales. That's an 8x growth rate! That wouldn't have happened if these hadn't been products people wanted. Still, Simon kept telling me the same thing. "You'll know when it's time to raise money. You'll know."

Then, after we got the normal wash in a few more Whole Foods stores, I got an unexpected email. It was from the feminine care buyer at Target, who was interested in learning more about our product and wanted to set up a meeting.

I forwarded the email to Simon.

"Now," he said. "Now we go raise money."

Chapter Six

When You Don't Know How, Do It Anyway

Pitching a vaginal care company to potential investors requires talking, mostly to men, about vaginas and vagina infections. A lot. It's not a topic that the guys at VC firms are generally comfortable discussing. I read an article recently in which one venture capitalist summed it up like this: "I don't want to talk about vaginas every Monday morning in my partner meeting." Cool.

If I wanted to take Honey Pot to the next level, not only did I have to convince these men that vaginal care was a market with growth and earnings potential, but I also had to get them used to discussing the subject matter, or even using the word. This was only one of many challenges when it came to raising money and scaling our business, but it was an additional one on top of the challenges all business owners face, and on top of my personal added challenges of being a woman, and a woman with brown skin.

I'll be honest, there were times when I was really scared of raising capital. You have to be a little bit crazy to think you can take something that has never existed before and make something out of nothing. To convince others you can do this? It takes guts. Plus, all my fear and trauma around growing up lower middle class and worrying about how others saw me as a Black woman would come flooding back anytime I had to talk about money. There's often an uncomfortable, unspoken power dynamic that goes on when a Black woman asks a room full of primarily white men for cash. But the truth is, my general hesitance around asking for money overshadowed any insecurities I had regarding who I was or how I looked. I wasn't thinking of myself as a Black woman. I was thinking of myself as Beatrice, who was taking a major chance by announcing to the world that this was what I wanted to do. The kind of money we needed, it was in numbers I'd never dealt with. We worked up to asking for investments of millions of dollars, and that felt like a shit ton of money! I have a more realistic perspective on those numbers now (it's not all that much in the business world), but at the time, I was intimidated by it. And yet, if you're in a pitch and you seem unsure of yourself, that comes through. If you don't believe in yourself, the men seated around the table certainly won't believe in you. So I entered those rooms as if I was the most confident woman in the world. Fake it till you make it, right?

The good news for any budding entrepreneur is that you only know what you know when you know it. If there was a way I was "supposed to" behave or talk or look, I didn't know it. When I started asking for money, I had no idea what mistakes I might make. I didn't know the complexities of taking on investments. I just knew that we absolutely needed financing, and that I would do whatever it took to get it.

... If you're in a pitch and you seem unsure of yourself, that comes through. If you don't believe in yourself, the men seated around the table certainly won't believe in you. So I entered those rooms as if I was the most confident woman in the world. Fake it till you make it, right?

Simon suggested that our first move, before entering any boardrooms or talking to any venture capitalists, should be to approach friends and family. Our first round of investments ultimately totaled $700,000, and we only asked people with whom we had connections, but asking for that money was just as difficult as asking for millions from white VC guys was later. It was completely new territory for me. One of the first people we approached was one of Sy's best friends. He lived in Boston but was in town for a visit, so we pitched him in Sy's living room. We put together a PowerPoint deck explaining what we were doing and where we thought we could take the company, but I had no idea what I was doing when I presented. I felt scared and embarrassed standing up there asking some guy I barely knew to give me his money. The cool thing, at least, was that he was willing to listen. I don't know if he ever had any intention of investing—and in the end he didn't give us any money—but he did give us good advice on how to tweak our pitch and what to include and what to ask for.

To us, our pitch was relatively straightforward and simple: Because we'd seen 8x growth after we added additional products to our website, we had the sales numbers to prove that making our own wipes and pads would be a viable business. Plus, we had interest from Target. That felt like a bird in the hand. This is one of the largest retailers in the United States, and they were interested in us! But pitching is never as easy as it should be. Potential investors asked for information we never even thought to gather. In those early days, we were desperate, and when that happens people can smell it. We pitched one guy who agreed to give us money but as a loan rather than an investment—meaning we *had* to pay it back, and in a designated time frame—but he also wanted equity in the company. That's a shit deal, and we knew it even then, but we had bills to pay. We owed the manufacturer who was making the product, and the design firm who did the packaging. We felt we had no choice but to say yes, but being on the hook to that guy almost broke us.

Another time we met with a businessman who didn't want

to invest, but he convinced us he could help us scale, and since we didn't have enough cash to pay him, we offered him equity in the company. Well, this guy did nothing for us. Eventually Sy said we had to ask for our equity back. We sat in the Gathering Spot, a coworking space in downtown Atlanta, for hours, and Sy begged him to do the right thing, but this man just looked us in the face and refused. "Nah," he said. "You gave me the equity and it's mine." What I know now is that when you are desperate and hungry and need money for your business, sometimes all you can see is the problem in front of you. But the decisions you make in those moments can stay with you for a long time. Sometimes you have to make a bad deal because you need to get to the next spot, but the more you're aware of this, the more you can protect yourself.

Other times we'd do a pitch and have multiple follow-up calls, and we'd bring them all the information they requested, like tax info or sales data, only for them to say, "I don't really do this type of business, I'm not comfortable." You get your hopes up and then nine times out of ten it's "I don't think it's a good fit." But then there are times when you meet with the right person at the right moment and it works out. We pitched another one of Sy's best friends, and it was like butter. We told her our story and she immediately said, "It's an undeniable yes." She gave us money that made a real difference to our business. Every now and then people saw what we did—that this was going to be big, and they wanted to be a part of it. But more often than not, it was a no.

Despite the frequent rejection, the great thing about that first round of money-raising was that we got practice. So much practice. I never thought about giving up, not ever, so my only choice was to get better. As far as I was concerned, this had to work out. There was no plan B for me. Sy would have been fine. He knew how to make money. He was a gifted CPA, and I didn't see a world in which he didn't succeed if he wanted to. But I wasn't sure that was the case for me. I didn't have a college degree. I'd had an unconventional career path that I knew others might judge. But that lit a wildfire under my ass to keep grinding. Simon and I were talking to people we (or mostly he) knew, and whether or not they invested, they would listen and then send us to the next person. The business world is all about introductions and connections, and we were pitching nonstop for months. Every single time, regardless of whether the person we were talking to had good intentions, we learned something. And we caught on quick. Each time we talked to a potential investor, we did a better job than the last time.

In that first pass, we raised nearly three-quarters of a million dollars. But let me back up a minute. The email I'd received was from a woman named Monique Benoit. It was sent to our customer support address, and I'd never been great about checking that inbox. One of our team members saw it first and sent me a text. "Hey, someone from Target reached out," he said. "You should check your email."

About six weeks earlier, I'd been having a conversation with

Linda, who asked me directly: "Who would be your ideal retail partner?"

"Easy," I said. "Target." So when I opened the email from Monique, the feminine care buyer in the company's over-the-counter department, I just about lost my mind. She had heard about our wash from her hairdresser, who had seen the product at the Bronner Bros. Hair Show. It's crazy to think how one thing always leads to the next, but I've learned that's how business works. It might seem like there's a secret sauce, and of course privilege and access and connections help some companies and some founders, but when your product is good and you're willing to keep hustling and you're doing it for the right reasons, I absolutely believe that the universe aligns for you.

The way Target worked back then was that after the initial email introduction, you'd do a fifteen-minute call with the buyer. On that call, Monique explained that she was working on a new initiative to "clean up" the shelves at Target. At that point, they only sold the conventional brands in the feminine care department, household names like Summer's Eve and Tampax. Monique was bringing in more products with clean, all-natural ingredients. I explained to her what made us different—not just our wash, which was made from plant-derived ingredients, but I explained the entire dream I had for what I believed vaginal wellness could be. I explained that we were going to branch into wipes and pads, all of which would be natural. We only had fifteen minutes, so I quickly took Monique through the numbers of what we'd been able to do on our own. We'd gotten our product into Whole Foods. We grew to just under $250,000 in sales in a single year. Imagine what we could do with the marketing budget of a major retailer? I'll never forget what she said to me next.

"Bea, if I bring you into Target, I need you to understand that what I'm going to ask you to do, it is almost impossible to do," she said. "Are you even up for that?"

I didn't hesitate for even a second. "Impossible is what I do."

I did everything I could to help Monique see our vision as a big-brand vaginal wellness company. If she could just get us to the next thing—which I knew by then would be a meeting at Target headquarters—I would not let her down. We could help her achieve her dream of cleaning up the shelves. If she gave us a chance to sit in front of her and show her the products and prove what we could do, we would convince her that we were the right partner.

She had to keep her poker face, even over the phone. When we hung up, I didn't know if we'd get invited to Minneapolis to pitch Target, but I knew I'd sold us as hard as I could. When I got the email inviting us to headquarters, I had all the feelings. I was crazy excited, because I was quite clear on how big an opportunity this was. Having our products carried in Target stores would be a gamechanger. But I was also intimidated. This was going to be a totally different ball game than pitching friends and family. There would be no second chances, no leeway because I was a friend of a friend. We had to get it right. It also meant that, if they took us, we'd have to change some of our business practices. My kitchen could no longer be our manufacturing plant, for example, because we'd have to produce more than just washes, and we'd have to do all of it in much larger amounts.

There was a lot to do to get ready for Minneapolis. I had a bit of a leg up thanks to my work as a food broker. I was literally getting brands into stores as my job, so I knew some of the ins and outs of how it worked. As a broker, I had to go into stores and know everything about the products I was trying to get placed. If I was trying get a buyer to order a specific jam, for example, I had to know all the ingredients of that jam and how it was different and better than the competitors. I was basically a salesperson. When it came to Honey Pot, knowing the product was the easy part. First of all, I'd been making it in my kitchen, by myself or with Antoinee, for years. I lived and breathed that wash. Plus, I believed in the brand more than I even believed in myself. You can't fake passion, and I had that in spades. But to place a product in Target, I also had to find a distributor that they would trust, because they needed to be confident that if they placed an order, the product would get to them in time. We had to hire a broker of our own, one who understood Target's product review schedule (what time of year they place their orders for different departments) and also what information they would need to see in our presentation to make their decision. I also wanted to be sure that I wasn't just showing our washes (we had sensitive and normal by then). We would start there, I figured, but I wanted Target to see the potential in us. I wanted it to be clear as day that putting us in their stores would translate to profits, because this is business and money talks. I wanted to present the whole vision. I wanted to showcase our commitment to following a consumer through her life cycle, and our determination to be the first company to cross the aisle between vaginal wellness and period care . . . even though we hadn't actually made those products yet.

There are two ways you can show a buyer a product that isn't created yet. You can create a prototype, or you can show a 3D render. A prototype is an early version of the actual product; a 3D render is ultimately just an image. It's a realistic image, certainly more than just a drawing, but still, it's an image. If you're in early stages and you're pitching a retailer where you don't already have shelf space, I can tell you right now that it's a mistake to show up with a 3D image. I knew that much because of my work experience. If we were a brand-new company and showed up to a Target meeting with just an image of the pads and wipes we *wanted* to make, they'd think we were wasting their time. How could we prove we could deliver a product if we didn't even have one to show?

I had never gotten a prototype made before, but this is when Google became my best friend. I typed in "I need prototypes of my products" and found a company called Rapid Prototypes. I reached out to them and explained that I had this big meeting and I wanted to be able to show an example of the wipes and pads that I wanted to make one day. I didn't even totally understand what I needed, but this is what they did every day, so it was all routine to them. I sent in bottles of our wash and samples from another wipe company and pad company, and they took the branding from our wash bottle and applied it to wipe and pad containers, and sent those containers to us in the mail. It all cost about $2,000 to make—money we didn't have just lying around—but it was worth it. We filled the boxes with tissues or other wipes since we didn't have our own, but the point was to have something physical to put in front of the buyers, so that they didn't have to imagine what we wanted to create. They could see it and hold it in their hands, and that was really powerful.

Target has a giant headquarters space in Minneapolis. Walking in and getting our badge—I was so nervous. I truly couldn't believe this was really happening. It wasn't so long ago that I'd called Target my "dream," and now here I was! It was the real deal, and I'd never spent much time in this kind of corporate environment. But as nervous as I was, I never felt like I couldn't do it. I never questioned my ability or the legitimacy of our company, so I showed up with our washes and prototypes and I pitched my heart out. It was easier than it should have been, because I lived and breathed Honey Pot. At the end of our pitch, after I'd walked through our vision and showed them the packaging for what I saw as our first collection, Monique was clearly taken aback. "Oh shit," she said. "You brought me a brand!"

She was exactly right. We were not a single product, and I wanted her to understand just how serious we were about our work and how dedicated we were to changing this category. Our vision was a good fit with Target, who was working to be the cool kids in mass market. They wanted to be the most innovative and carry the hippest brands. Clean beauty was what was cool—new feminine care brands weren't launching unless they were organic or natural, and our company was plant-derived feminine care. Target told us they wanted the washes and also the wipes, and they wanted to carry them in eleven hundred stores nationwide. Until then, we'd only been sold in local Atlanta retailers. It was the dream.

To fulfill Target's order, we needed money. That's where the family and friends came in. And if we wanted to actually stay on the shelves . . . we needed even more cash. We weren't just fundraising so we could gradually scale anymore. We needed investments, and we needed them now. We were going to need to hire a bigger team, which meant we needed money for payroll. We also needed to be able to fulfill orders on a weekly basis. Simon was right to stop us from fundraising before the Target email, because if you don't have tangible plans for growth, investors will eat you alive. But now we were in a different situation.

As we transitioned from talking to friends and family to talking to investment firms, the conversations got even more complicated. I remember pitching one firm and feeling so good about our preparation. We gave them the hard press and it went really well! Then they were like, "Great, can you give us access to your data room?" Blank stares. We had no idea what a data room was. I know now that a data room is a virtual space where you put all your company data—your sales, the numbers regarding what's happening in the retail space, your tax information, basically everything you need to run your business on a year-to-year basis—but I didn't know any of that at the time. We were learning, every single day.

Then there was the vagina piece. I have never shuddered or giggled or cringed at the word *vagina*. I have never whispered it as if I was talking about something inappropriate or offensive. I talk about the female body with the respect it deserves. Everyone on this planet got here thanks to a penis and a vagina. Two people had sex, or one person jerked off and it went into a tube, or whatever. It's not rocket science. It's literally how humanity always has and always will repopulate, unless people are getting cloned in the future, so it shouldn't be all that hard to talk about. But as we started meeting with bigger investors, we weren't always met with that same level of comfort around body talk. And while my ultimate goal was to normalize conversations around vaginas and vaginal care, when Sy and I met with potential investors, our approach was to meet them where they were. No one wants a lecture, and we were trying to solicit their money, so we wanted to stay on their good side. Instead, we tried to lighten up the topic and make it feel more approachable. We didn't speak in hushed tones. We reminded the people we were speaking to that even if they don't have a vagina—and most of them did not—they were familiar with them. Someone in their life was affected by vaginal care. They had a wife or girlfriend or daughter or sister. Keep in mind, about 85 percent of venture capitalists are men. And generally, humans want to invest in what they know.

I was already coming in as something of an underdog—in 2023, companies with a female founder only got about 20 percent of all venture capital funding (companies with exclusively female founders only got 2 percent). In 2016, when I was pitching investors, those numbers were even lower. Black-founded companies are also underfunded. In 2022, 1 percent of funding went to companies with Black founders; even less, probably, in 2016. When investors are trying to decide where to invest their money, they look for comps. They want to see companies with a similar leadership profile that have already gotten funding and had success—they use it as proof that their investment can see a return. If investors are considering funding your company, but when they look around at the marketplace they don't see other people like you doing similar work, they are going to value you less because they haven't seen it done before. There haven't been enough Black women who've done what I'm doing, so on paper I probably looked to them like a bigger risk. Needless to say, all the odds were stacked against me, and now I was coming into these rooms talking about vulva care, of all things. Plus, VC firms these days are mostly hearing about tech brands—even the companies that aren't tech are positioning themselves as tech. These founders usually come in the room ready to talk data and use all the colorful tech lingo you need when raising capital. I wasn't quite there yet. I had sales numbers, but Honey Pot is not a tech brand. We are a human brand. We sell packaged goods. We make tangible products you will buy in a grocery aisle. I wasn't about to pretend we were something we are not.

I can't be anything but who I am, so I also wasn't walking into rooms spouting business jargon I didn't understand. I was just showing up as me. I looked how I look and I spoke how I speak. I am not the typical businesswoman, I know that. Or at least, I don't present like one. I have tattoos on my face. A *fuck* or a *shit* might come out of my mouth at any moment. There are usually cultural differences in these rooms, and whether consciously or not, that absolutely affects which companies get money and which do not. If you are a Black business owner, you have to go in knowing that you're going to face extra obstacles. It's just the reality. But I don't think very much about the fact that I'm Black or that I'm a woman, because the color of my skin and what's between my legs should not matter.

While there are a lot of inherent problems with the idea that investors like to invest in what they know—at least in a world where investors largely look a certain way—at a human level, I can understand it. If we're talking about someone who has built his own wealth, it's natural that he wants to invest in areas where he is comfortable and confident. And even at investment firms, these groups usually represent high-net-worth individuals. People are putting their money at risk. They want to have a sense of where that money is going, and they want to have something to offer the company that's using it. My goal in these rooms became to prove to these guys that, actually, this company *is* focused on something they know.

It often went something like this.

Me: "Honey Pot is a company that makes vaginal washes. We provide a healthy alternative to conventional feminine care that's free of parabens, carcinogens, and sulfates. Our wash healed me when I suffered from bacterial vaginosis, and now it has healed our many customers. Sales are growing. Infections like BV and yeast infections are more common than you think, and even for those who don't have an infection, our solution provides natural and proactive vulva care."

Them: "Uh, well, we don't really know about vaginas."

Me: "But you do!"

The suspicion and confusion they tended to feel was palpable.

The pitch, which I still stand behind today, was that if you are a heterosexual cis man in America, you have come into contact with a vagina. First of all, we all came from one. There's nothing weird about that, it's just life. Also, I'd explain, you can probably remember a moment when a woman you care about was dealing with a vaginal issue or you had to run out and buy a tampon or pad or medicine for her. You know what it's like to be in bed with a woman who feels confident and comfortable down there, and what it's like to be with someone who is shy or embarrassed because she's worried that there's something to hide. It wasn't that these guys were making sexist or stupid jokes about lady parts; they just didn't feel comfortable investing their money in something they felt unfamiliar with. I was there to make them realize that I was addressing an issue that people need products for every single month, if not every day. People are not going to stop taking showers. They are not going to stop getting their periods. I was there to ground these investors in reality and, when necessary, get them out of their man brain. We didn't try to make it clinical or weird, we just said, *Think about your own experiences. This actually isn't as foreign to you as you might think.*

Given all that I had working against me, including being a double minority and the fact that there were barely any African-American female founders who'd raised millions of dollars for me to use as comps, talking about vaginas in pitch meetings should have been the least of my concerns. And in most ways, it was. I was much more concerned about where the money would come from than I was about men feeling *icky* about women's body parts. But at the same time, it represented my broader mission. I want to empower humans with vaginas, and that means destigmatizing vaginas. It means talking about them with respect. It means talking about them honestly, like they are human organs, rather than whispering and giggling or using only euphemisms. It means acknowledging their power and vulnerabilities, just like my mother taught me to do. But that has to come from all humans, not just those *with* vaginas. Because if you have a sore throat, you're probably going to talk to someone about it. If you break your leg, you're going to get it fixed. If you can't see the words on the page when you're reading a book, you're probably going to get your eyes checked, and maybe get glasses. Healing your vagina should be no different, but it starts with feeling safe to speak your truth out loud.

It's hard to say if mine was a winning pitch. We got many more nos than yeses, but that's pretty much always the case, no matter what your business is. It felt like winning to me in that it got people more comfortable having the conversations I needed to be having. And it must have been winning, because ultimately we raised the money we needed to fulfill our commitment to Target and get our products on the shelves. But were there more hard moments than not? Absolutely! And while I had the mental fortitude, in each hard moment, to dust myself off and keep going, I won't pretend I didn't get disappointed or angry or frustrated. There were plenty of times when we were invited to pitch a firm and I thought, *OK, they asked us to come, they're definitely going to invest. This is going to be the break we've been waiting for.* And then when the subsequent rejection came, I was heartbroken. There was one private equity fund in particular that I believed would be the perfect partner for us. Not just because they had the money we needed, but also because they could guide us and

> I want to empower humans with vaginas, and that means destigmatizing vaginas. It means talking about them with respect.

help take us to the next level. We pitched a few partners from this firm at Expo West, a major trade show focused specifically on natural and organic products. We had what I hoped would be our first of many meetings, mostly to start building relationships, but soon afterward I got a call from my contact that their advisory board didn't feel like we were a good fit. I was devastated—I strongly believed that Honey Pot was heading in the same direction as their portfolio companies—but I couldn't wallow. I had to put on a brave face and explain to these folks why I thought they were making a huge mistake. I wanted them to understand how passionate I was not just about Honey Pot but also about a potential partnership. They were kind and they listened, but they didn't change their minds.

And then there was another brand that was doing something similar to Honey Pot at the time, focusing specifically on clean menstrual products, and that company was raising millions and millions of dollars. They were online only, yet they seemed to be having an easier time than us—even though we were about to go into one of the biggest mass-market retailers in the world. When I thought about it too long, I was flabbergasted. And pissed! *How are they raising so much capital when it is so hard for us? We already have a yes from Target, why is this so difficult?* Those were the same moments when I would think to myself, *Shit, if we were white this would have been a lot easier.* But at the same time, it was like, fuck it. We don't have time to bemoan this, we've got to get to the next thing. We kept pushing because that's all you can do.

But some good came of our desperation, too. We got so many

nos, sometimes for fair reasons that had to do with our projections, other times because of more deep-seated reservations that had to do with racism and bigotry and sexism and the inability to take a "vagina company" seriously. But our turnaround was so tight that I didn't have time to wallow. I couldn't get caught up in the rejections because I had shit to do and money to raise. The day-to-day operations of Honey Pot did not pause while we were pitching investors and asking for money, which means that we were still creating products and selling them in stores and online and operating all aspects of our business. It was all work all the time. I didn't eat, I didn't sleep. I was working sixty-plus-hour weeks and there still weren't enough hours in the day. And all this was happening while Sy and I were still working our day jobs. He had an office for his tax practice, and sometimes we would use that space for calls and meetings, but my kitchen was still our laboratory, and during the day I was still working as a food broker. Luckily I worked from home for that job when I wasn't on the road, and I mostly owned my time, so I could get away with juggling two gigs at once. But it wasn't easy. Not even close. I remember one day I was on the road in Nashville with a new food broker I was training. She was driving us from one store to the next, and I was in the passenger seat fielding calls the whole time. I was talking to Sy and we were following up with an investor who had guaranteed us they were going to give us some cash. Then, over the phone, the investor bailed. I don't remember why or what reason he gave for changing his mind, I just remember hanging up the phone and screaming in the car, loudly, and then bursting into tears. I apologized to this trainee, and she just had to keep driving! That's what it was like, each day. I was doing a thousand things at once. I wasn't balancing two jobs—there was no *balance* involved—I was just doing more than I reasonably should have. During the daytime I was food brokering and fielding investment calls, while Antoinee was in my kitchen making the wash. Once I could clock out of my nine-to-five for the day, she and I would pack orders—bottling, wrapping, packaging, shipping. There was a post office near my place that was open really late and we were always the last people in line for the day. Those postal workers hated seeing us coming, because we always showed up right when they were about to close. I was paying for all of this in terms of exhaustion and stress—getting up early and working late into the night—but we were moving into Target, and I was not about to screw that up.

There is a secret power to being an underdog, because it forces you to believe in yourself. Well, you can believe in yourself or you can give up, and I was not about to do the latter.

Plus, I had employees to pay, and I felt the weight of that. Owing someone else their living wage means you can't take any decisions lightly. It's not just you who will be affected if your cash runs out. We didn't have time to focus on those who didn't want to invest in us because I had to find the people who did. And I can say with complete honesty that I am so grateful for every one of those nos, because I don't want to be in bed with the wrong people. I don't want to be beholden to someone who truly believes that because I have a vagina I'll be too emotional some days to lead a company. Once someone invests in your business, they do not go away. And if they think little of you at the beginning, that is not going to change, even if you make them their money back and then some.

While raising money, Simon and I were underestimated at every turn. But there is a secret power to being an underdog, because it forces you to believe in yourself. Well, you can believe in yourself or you can give up, and I was not about to do the latter. Everything about scaling a business when you don't really know what you're doing comes down to the same thing: You just keep going. It's uncomfortable, it's hard, it's stressful. You are selling yourself and asking for money, and that might feel unfamiliar and awkward, but you do it anyway. A little fear and insecurity is healthy. It keeps you just humble enough, because it takes a special person to want to bring something into the world that will improve lives. And no matter who you are, if you are trying to do something that's never been done before, people are going to be skeptical. It's not always intentional, and it doesn't always come from a bad place. In fact, it probably comes from a reasonable place—if no one's done this before, why should they believe *you* will. So you convince them. You say to yourself, *This is weird, I wish I didn't have to do it*, and then you ask for what you need in spite of all that. It's a business lesson I learned fairly quickly. In my personal life, it took a bit longer.

Chapter Seven

Choose You

In 2014, the same year that Honey Pot launched at the Bronner Bros. Hair Show, I got married. The growth of the relationship in many ways mirrored the growth of Honey Pot. As I've mentioned, we dated long-distance during the same years that I was battling BV, years where I was going through it emotionally, physically, and spiritually. As I've said, it was a time defined mostly by searching. Searching for physical comfort, searching for professional purpose, searching for spiritual fulfillment, and searching for personal connection. By 2014, I was tired of searching and wanted to lock it all in. All these parts of my life felt like they were on the cusp of becoming something big and real, and I just wanted to get there already.

In many ways, the relationship was doomed from the start. I wasn't in the right mental state for a healthy romance. When we started dating, I was unhappy with my life and with myself, and while I truly believed I loved this person, I know now that you can't love somebody else if you don't love yourself. The dynamics of our relationship were complicated, but in the simplest terms I would say that he was addicted to being in charge, and I was addicted to being of service. And in fact, because I was feeling so overwhelmed in my life, being controlled felt like being taken care of. His control felt like love, and so I dedicated an enormous amount of energy to serving this man and proving that I was worthy of whatever it was he was giving.

When you are urgently seeking something, you are going to find it. And when you act from a place of romantic desperation, you take what you can get. That's not the right time to be looking for love. (It's not unlike what I learned about raising money for a business—desperate times lead to desperate measures and all that.) I attracted precisely what I got, which was a relationship that wasn't healthy and didn't make me feel good about myself, even if I couldn't see that in the moment.

By the time this man and I got married, it was as if I'd added another job on top of running Honey Pot and being a food broker. Being his wife was work—I was working to maintain the relationship, to prove that I loved him enough and in the right ways, to show my gratitude for him being there. In a healthy partnership, time with the other person should feel like a break from work. They should be the respite. The relationship should feel good. There should be an ease to it, even if it isn't always easy. There should be comfort. But my marriage was not that. It was not a place of relaxation. We weren't right for each other, so being married meant I was working, literally, 24/7. It added complexity to my life because it was another thing I was trying to solve for. And while the Honey Pot solutions were hard-earned but always felt *right* and *destined*, the work of my marriage felt like labor that bore no fruit. The business was growing, but my relationship was, in many ways, diminishing.

The pace of business at Honey Pot could have, maybe even should have, been a positive distraction from the pain of my marriage. After all, at this point I was eating, breathing, sleeping Honey Pot. It also could have demanded so much attention that I failed to notice the dysfunction of my relationship. But the truth is, for me, there was no separation. My professional work and my personal life, even now, they are all one thing. Which meant that the labor of Honey Pot and the labor of my relationship all jumbled together so that I couldn't always identify the source of my stress or the deep unhappiness I was feeling. I would be sharp or defensive with someone at work, or I'd insist on being right, and I thought it was because building a company required that level of intensity. I chalked it up to the entrepreneur's hamster wheel. Honey Pot certainly required my time and energy, but could it have been a more joyful experience in the beginning? Maybe. I will never know. And, if I hadn't been so involved with work, might I have realized earlier how unhappy I was in my relationship? Also, maybe.

At some point during our marriage, I thought I wanted to

get pregnant. We didn't try for a super long time, but it was long enough that at some point I went to the doctor to get my levels checked and make sure everything was in working order. I wanted to be sure that I *could* get pregnant, eventually. Perhaps unsurprisingly, between a toxic relationship and the strain of trying to build a business, my entire body was out of whack. I was experiencing pH imbalances, I was majorly overweight, and my cortisol and stress levels were through the roof. For the past few years I had been steadfastly avoiding the doctor because I was scared of what I might learn. I knew I was working myself to the bone and not taking good care of my body, and I didn't want to hear that my cholesterol was high or my hormones were off. I was terrified that I was sick and if I was, I didn't want to know it. But it was at that appointment—for which my mother joined me—that I learned that my thyroid levels were elevated.

> Being seen, especially in moments of vulnerability, is comforting but it's also scary. It forces you to face truths you've been trying to hide from.

My mom and I got into the car after the appointment, ready to drive the forty minutes back to my home. That's when she said it: "What are you lying about?"

"What are you talking about?" I said.

"Beatrice. We don't have thyroid problems in our family," she said. "For you to develop one out of nowhere, you are lying to yourself about something."

I had never said it out loud, but deep down, I knew what I was lying about. I'd been living a lie for years—telling myself I was happy, or at least content, in a relationship that wasn't working. I was working late into the nights on Honey Pot business because I needed to, but also because it was easier to avoid my personal life in the name of work than it was to face it. I was telling the people who cared about me that my marriage was going well, that I was thriving, that I was happy at home, when in fact, behind closed doors, everything was hard and unpleasant and unhealthy.

But that day, my mother saw me. Being seen, especially in moments of vulnerability, is comforting but it's also scary. It forces you to face truths you've been trying to hide from. I burst into tears in that car because I could no longer live in denial. I couldn't pretend I didn't see what was happening. It was as if I'd been living for years with a frog in my throat—I needed to just say the truth, but I couldn't get it out—and this conversation was forcing me to face my choices and my reality. "Any day you live doing *anything* you don't want to do, it's time wasted." My mother's words came at me with more force than any of the cars on that Atlanta highway. "We could drive home right now and get hit by a truck. Would you be OK to die right now? On your deathbed, would you be OK with the decisions that you have made?"

Her words were not unlike the words of my grandmother that morning in my dream, trying to force my eyes open so I could get to work and heal myself. It was a shout: "Wake up!!!!"

When my mother leveled with me, putting it as bluntly as

possible that I only had this one life and that every day I spent living a lie was a day I spent as good as dead, I really did wake up. I opened my eyes to my own mortality, which ultimately got me to leave that marriage, and to choose myself and my happiness. It didn't happen immediately, but my mother's words rattled around inside my head until one day, during a different car ride, the man I was married to said something that finally made it all click. I don't even remember exactly what it was, except I certainly remember that it made me think, once and for all: *What am I doing? Why am I here? How can I bring children into the world in a relationship that is this unhealthy? How much more time can I waste?*

When I finally realized what I needed to do, I needed to do it *immediately*. The car ride with my husband ended like a scene out of the movies. We were en route to see some family, and I gripped my hands on the wheel and busted a U-turn out of nowhere, in the middle of traffic, changing course both literally and figuratively. By then my mother's message had seeped into my bones. Every day I continued to live that lie was a day wasted. Until I could live my truth, I was as good as dead. In that moment, I took control of the direction of my life.

Getting divorced takes time, so my marriage wasn't immediately dissolved, but after that car ride, we parted ways. And guess what? I'm not saying that every illness is an indicator or that there's a 1:1 correlation—sometimes a person just gets sick and it's bad luck and it's shitty and I would never place blame—but there are times when our pain or medical issues really do act as an alert system to something deeper or bigger going on, and that can be a real service. That's what was happening in my case.

When I indulge in the retelling of my marriage, and all the little moments that led to its demise, it can come off as an exercise in blame. It's not a good look on me, and it's not good for my soul. I don't want to swim in those waters anymore. Because here's the truth: Everything that happened was my decision. No one forced me into a relationship against my will. I was responsible for all of it. I wasn't treated well, but I don't blame anybody but myself, because I accepted the treatment, and I walked into that relationship with my eyes wide open. There were warning signs that I absolutely could have heeded, but I chose to ignore them. There were things that weren't my fault, but I believe the onus is on me. I chose not to register them at all, because we see what we want to see. For a long time, I was afraid to leave, and so I stayed.

Fear, exhaustion, stress, but also determination and drive and hustle, they can prevent you from seeing what is right in front of you.

Telling a story of the past, *my* story, can also come off as a tale of "shoulda, woulda, coulda." I can look back and pinpoint so many times when I should have done something else: walked away, stayed home, said no. But "should have" doesn't matter, and it's a fruitless exercise. We make our own choices. We live with them.

My divorce fucked me up for a long while, not only because

of the man I was married to but because every time I reflected on the marriage, I had to sit with the knowledge that I allowed myself to suffer those experiences. There's a real shame that comes from that. I had to forgive myself, and it wasn't easy.

As I see it today, mine isn't really a story of divorce. It's a story of discovery. When I think about my marriage, what I think about is not any particular argument or conflict. What I think about doesn't even involve the man I was with at all. I chose a path and he was a part of it, but the story is not about him. It's about the depths to which I was so busy serving others—my husband, my colleagues, my company—that I forgot myself. It's about the levels of blindness I willingly let myself sit in. Fear, exhaustion, stress, but also determination and drive and hustle, they can prevent you from seeing what is right in front of you.

My marriage and subsequent divorce taught me a lot about relationships and what I wanted to look for in the future. I know now what it's like to be in a toxic relationship. I know what it feels like to be with someone who is trying to control me. I can sense it in my gut and my soul. And in moments when I have found myself in relationships that weren't serving me, I've checked myself real fast. Because control is not love. It took me an incredibly long time to acknowledge this lesson that now seems so painfully obvious. When it comes to my life, only I belong in the driver's seat.

Chapter Eight

Excellence Is Baseline

"We want to put Honey Pot in eleven hundred stores across the country," Monique told me over the phone. "But to do that, you need to have product ready for shelves in less than a year. It won't be easy."

It didn't seem like very much time, but the reality was that any extra time was a blessing. Originally Target was only going to stock us in 250 stores. Had that been the case, they would have needed product (that we didn't have!) right away. When they reconsidered and grew the order to 1100 stores—far more than most brands get out of the gate from a mass retailer—they told us that we'd have to wait longer to be on the shelves. A lot of companies in our boat would have wanted immediate distribution because they needed the sales, but we needed time above all else. All things in order! The delay was welcome, and over the coming months, I worked like a horse. There was so much to do. To start, we needed to produce exponentially more product, so we had to transition the formulation of our washes from my kitchen to a mass production facility. We also had to reconsider some of our ingredients. Sandalwood, for example, was affordable when we were buying it on a small scale, but for mass production it would have made the wash too expensive. We also had to create the wipes that thus far only existed in prototype form. That required finding a company to manufacture them and negotiating that pricing. At the time, we were selling a different company's wipes on our site, and I remember hoping that this company would tell me who their manufacturer was, but when I asked, they didn't volunteer the info. So, back to Google I went.

Of course, plenty of manufacturers had no interest in working with us. We were still a small company, with no guarantee of continued orders. We'd call and inquire about their pricing and they'd basically say, *You're tiny, no thank you.* A lot of manufacturers have minimum order quantities, or MOQs, and you can't even look in their direction unless you're producing millions of units per year. Then, when we finally did get a manufacturer, we had to go through several iterations to find the right feel and the right smell for the wipe. On top of all that, we also had to create our branding. Up until then we had basic packaging, but now we needed better messaging and a clever tagline and a beautiful website with stunning photos. And branding is expensive! We ended up going with a smaller, newer agency because it's what we could afford—but because they, like us, were just starting out, we needed to leave more room for error and accept that everything would take a little bit longer.

Needless to say, it was one foot in front of the other. The minute we solved one problem, there was only one question: "What's next?"

In 2017, our products hit shelves in 1,100 Target stores, and sales gradually built up. We launched with our two washes—normal and sensitive—and our newly created feminine wipes. Not long afterward, we created a line of herbal pads and panty liners that we got in the doors of 50 Targets. They became a fly-off-the-shelves bestseller. I like to call them an air conditioner for the vagina, because with herbs like lavender and mint, they're incredibly refreshing. Within twelve months of launching in Target, we went from being a vulva wash company to becoming a full-fledged feminine care brand.

Of course, the launch was not without its challenges. It was hard to keep our products in stock (good problem to have!) because we were scaling at such a rapid rate. Early on, we encountered an issue with our wipes that I worried was going to take us out. Whenever you make a product, you have to put it through what's called microtesting. This involves analyzing products for microbial contamination. It's basically quality control, and all our products passed microtesting before we stocked them on the shelves. Not too long after entering Target, however, we got a message from a customer that our wipes had a terrible smell. It wasn't simply that she didn't enjoy the smell, she said, it was that they smelled rotten. We got more information from this customer—namely the lot number that her package came from—and went to the store and bought a few packages to check out. The minute we opened one of them, it was obvious she wasn't exaggerating. The wipes smelled putrid. We had to go through every box of product in our warehouse, and open hundreds of cases, and remove all the tainted ones. The wipes had passed micro, but an ingredient must have gone rancid. Luckily they weren't all bad, and we could identify the tainted ones from their lot number, but that was an arduous and hard undertaking. Plus we had to pull the contaminated packs from stores nationwide. We worked tirelessly to avoid a recall, and it was a horrible few weeks, but we got through it. On the bright side, that incident forced us to develop even stricter protocols around how we handled microtesting. I'm relieved to say that never happened again.

Despite these difficulties, launching in Target was a gamechanger for Honey Pot. Pretty soon, that check hanging on my ceiling went from a dream to a reality. We hit the million-dollar sales goal, which was simultaneously exciting and completely uneventful. (I should point out that while I wrote the check on my ceiling to myself, it represented money for Honey Pot—it wasn't as if I personally pocketed a million dollars within a year of being in Target.) It was exciting, because I knew that my life and company were on their way to abundance. I could see that our work was paying off, and our vision was becoming a reality. That sales marker was the first major goal I'd set for Honey Pot, so to be able to say "we did it" felt good. But at the same time, our company was growing fast and just trying to keep up with demand, so there wasn't a lot of time to sit in that achievement or celebrate it. And when you are creating and growing a business, while profit is critical—you literally cannot survive without it—the intense work required is only manageable if you're working toward something larger than a monetary goal. You need to have passion for, and find purpose in, the work. Otherwise the money will never be enough.

I've never been particularly good at celebrating Honey Pot's milestones or achievements. In part, that's because there is always more work to be done. My team and I are always head down, trying to stay one step ahead. We are paying attention to FDA regulations and wellness trends. We play in every regulatory system there is—over-the-counter-drugs, medications, non-medicated treatments—and there's a real art to that. It's not easy and it takes focus. But the other reason I tend not to celebrate is that I expect nothing less than excellence. It's the level at which I presume Honey Pot will operate at all times. As far as I'm concerned, excellence is homeostasis. This doesn't mean there isn't margin for error or failure, but if I am going to put my time and energy into something, I expect it to go well. If we are not striving for greatness, if we are not trying to make the absolute best product possible, then what are we doing? What's the point otherwise? It would be downright disrespectful if we didn't go out of our way to do everything we can to make the best washes and pads and wipes that we can make in order to serve the most people we can and ultimately make the most money we can. It's why we're here. Sometimes that comes with accolades, but I don't expect a medal for doing what I set out to do. Sure, it's nice to get your flowers, but when we make a million dollars or get a major investment or have a successful launch, I am not thinking, *Wow, we did it.* I am thinking: *This was the expectation. This is why we are here. We can't pat ourselves on the back for doing what we set out to do. That's just baseline.* If we have a win, that's great, but it's because we put in the work.

> I may try to change the world around me, something I hope I'm doing as a Black woman leading a now multimillion-dollar business, but I'm not about to sit around and whine. I'm going to put my head down and do the work.

It's important to note, also, that when you're a Black-owned, female-founded business, that margin for error is a little bit smaller. Because of the state of the society we live in, our team at Honey Pot cannot mess around. I don't know how to be anything but who I am. If I'm sad and you ask me how I'm doing, I'm going to say I'm sad; if you catch me in a moment of abundance, I'll say that too. But when I show up in a meeting or an interview as my authentic self, there will be people who see me and hear me and, as a result, underestimate me. Because of that, the work has to speak for itself. We don't have the luxury of certain privileges that many, even most, other start-ups have—connections or commonalities that can give some companies run by white men a leg up. That sometimes means my team and I have to work ten times harder than most other businesses. But I'm fine with that—it's the world we live in and I'm not scared of hard work. I'm also not someone who is going to complain about the state of things. I may try to change the world around me, something I hope I'm doing as a Black woman leading a now multimillion-dollar business, but I'm not about to sit around and whine. I'm going to put my head down and do the work.

Despite all the success Honey Pot saw after landing in Target, perhaps the most meaningful and life-changing outcome of the deal was a personal one: I could finally afford to quit my food broker day job to focus on running Honey Pot full-time.

Working for only myself felt like the truest version of freedom. Of course, in reality, I work for so many other people: our customers, most importantly, who drive and inspire everything I do, and our investors, who gave us money because they believed in our potential but also, at the end of the day, because they expect to earn their investment back and make money on top of it. I never forget that I answer to these groups. They are vitally important to me, as is the team of now seventy-five humans that Honey Pot employs all over the country. But getting to say that I was working exclusively toward my own vision, my own dream, rather than someone else's, was a pivotal moment for me.

It's very popular these days to say you want to be an entrepreneur. It's glamorized on TikTok and Instagram and TV shows, but a lot of people like the idea of being a business owner more than they would ever enjoy the work in practice. Some people need a nine-to-five job. They want to go in to work, do what's asked of them, and then go home. And more power to them! I am not someone who believes that everyone needs to live and breathe their professional life, and I can see the appeal of having a clear separation between work and home.

Being an entrepreneur is empowering and liberating but it's also a lot of pressure. In the business world, you're only as good as your last deal, and then you need to find more bread. That hustle isn't for everyone. But entrepreneurship was ingrained in me from the moment I was old enough to leave the house by myself. I like going out and having to find my food. It's the only way I know how to operate.

As Honey Pot has continued to grow, I often find myself in panel conversations or interviews or presentations, and there's one inquiry in particular that I hear on repeat: *Did you ever imagine that your company would be so big?* I'm not sure why it's always asked with a tinge of shock, but it's usually clear that the questioner is the one who can hardly believe it. Maybe because it's a female-focused company. Maybe because it was originally built to serve vaginas specifically. To say that this area of wellness hasn't always been taken seriously would be a vast understatement. The simple fact that people always ask *can you believe it?* is a sign of how far we still have to go. Half the population has a vagina, yet people seem shocked that a company that started by catering to that organ can have such success.

I always knew what we had. There has never been a millisecond of time that I questioned what Honey Pot is or what it could be—not since I used that first bottle of wash on myself. Honey Pot has been like a second religion for me. It is one of the gods that I serve. I believed in it and knew it was real even if I couldn't see it in front of me. When you have the desire to create and you know that you're onto something, you have to inject a level of belief in it the same way you have to inject belief into any kind of spirituality you practice. You have to do it before you see it. I had to be an evangelist for this company, and I could do that because my business was the one aspect of my life that I felt I had complete control over. It was the one that I could steer and influence. My romantic relationship was floundering. My body was still trying to right itself. But Honey Pot came from my ancestors! It was bestowed upon me, and I knew I could make it or break it with my own hard work. I had a sense of ownership in this one area of my life that I simply didn't have in others, and that alone was a gift. To feel a sense of power and agency in any area of your life, especially when things are hard, is a blessing.

And while hard work was absolutely the driving force in Honey Pot's growth, some of it was divine. Even in our toughest moments, building this business felt like when you are driving in the city and there's a traffic light every mile and you hit that stretch where you keep catching the green light. I wasn't always the happiest person and I was stressed and carrying a lot and I had to rely on my sheer belief in myself and the work it took was insane and and and . . . but it was working. Whatever it was that made people connect to this product, it was catching like wildfire. When I took a step back, the momentum was undeniable, pretty much from day one. Of course there were obstacles like a motherfucker, and as we grew after the Target launch, the obstacle course got bigger. We still had to make payroll and create new products and ensure inventory got to stores on time and in good shape, but now we also needed to know, for example, how to deal with ambulance-chasing attorneys and when it was time to discontinue a product. On the plus side, the more successful you are the better able you are to hire the right people—people who are way smarter than you and have done this obstacle course before, and if they haven't, they know someone who has. No matter what has gone wrong for us, there has always been a path to the next thing.

So, yes, I knew we would be successful. I was confident that we would see that million in sales, but I also knew that a million was just a number. It signified success because it took so long to reach and because I'd set my sights on it three years earlier, but I always knew that if we could make a million, then we could make ten million, and if we could make ten we could make a hundred, and then five hundred, and then a billion dollars. There is no limit as far as I'm concerned, but we have to earn it.

Soon after landing in Target, we added Walmart and Walgreens and Kroger and CVS to our list of retailers. As these wins piled up, I had to reconsider how I defined success. I knew it wasn't just a sales number anymore, but I couldn't pinpoint what a successful end looked like. How could I know when I'd "made it"?

On one hand, I've always felt, from day one, that Honey Pot has already made it. We made it when we gave our products away in parking lots and people came back reporting that they were healed. We made it when we sold out in a weekend at the Hair Show. We made it when I saw my wash on a shelf at Whole Foods, then at Target. We sell to human beings who trust us with their most personal and sensitive parts, and I have never taken that responsibility lightly. It's important to me to help our customers understand their bodies. To make them feel better in their bodies. I want all humans with vaginas to be aware of, or at least to be investigating, why they use the products they do. I want the world to understand that it really is important, for example, to use an organic pad or tampon, even if it's not my company's organic pad or tampon. Creating that level of consciousness is certainly a form of making it.

But success in business is also about money. It just is. The day Simon and I decided to raise money for our company and take on investors was the day we declared publicly and steadfastly that this business was not a hobby. It was not a passion project. If that's how someone else approaches their company, that's their business. That's great for them. But when we decided to take on investments, we knew we were getting involved with people who expected to get ten dollars back for every one that they invested. That is why they put money into our company. Sure, they might also believe in our mission or want to support us as a business owners, but they also might not. It might all be about the bottom line, and that's OK. Our investors don't need some noble reason to invest in us. It's their money! They worked hard for it and earned it, so if they are giving it to us, we understand the expectations and responsibility that come along with that. The minute we decided to take on VC money, we had to have an exit in mind, because we owed it to the people who gave us that lifeline just as much as we owed it to ourselves.

There's a long-enduring myth that to care about profit or focus on the dollars makes you greedy or inauthentic. That if you care about money, you must not care about your customers. Or if you focus on the bottom line, then you've ditched your mission and sold your soul. In Black culture especially—and even more specifically for Black women—building a business with the intention of making a profitable exit is often seen as selling out. There's a stigma around it, but I've been very vocal about how problematic that line of thinking can be. There should be no shame associated with taking an exit package or selling a company. If we want to create wealth, maybe even generational wealth, we need to make the big moves. Wealth is not created by toiling away 24/7 for years on end. It's created by finding and executing an exit. And if you can achieve that, it's not just that you will have a fat check in your wallet. Money is how you can make positive generational change and give back to your community and break cycles. Money creates power.

Financial wellness matters. In the world we live in, money is a requirement like food and water and air. We need it to survive and thrive, and anything that I need in order to live my fullest life, I take that seriously. I give it respect, because I acknowledge its importance, and I reject the idea that there is any selfishness or dishonor in wanting to get your due, or in wanting to live well. If you are devoting your time and effort and energy to putting work into the world, it should pay you. That's what business is for—making money. If we reject that in our community while other cultures thrive on that very same system, we aren't doing our part to help break cycles and lift up our own.

The minute my team stops putting love and devotion into that work is the minute we begin to fail. And failure is not an option.

Making an impact without making a profit is not a viable end for Honey Pot. But neither is making a fortune without helping or healing our customers. The good news is that we don't have to choose. I can be a compassionate, conscious, and successful businessperson. I have given all my energy to this company, and because I need to eat and live and support my family, it needs to pay me. But I have always believed that if I am building this company right, the money will come. I am not going to sell my soul in exchange for the bread, and even more importantly, the company is not going to sell its soul. I am doing this work, above all else, to help people liberate themselves and take care of themselves. The minute my team stops putting love and devotion into that work is the minute we begin to fail. And failure is not an option.

Chapter Nine

Building Community Through Crisis

"Hey, how are you holding up?"

"You good?"

Text messages like these—tons of them—were blowing up my phone and I didn't know why. They were mostly from people I rarely spoke to, so I knew something had to be up, though I had no idea what. Eventually, a close friend—one who knows I'm rarely on social media—told me to check the Honey Pot accounts, and there it was: an outpouring of hate. Trolls upon trolls were determined to take us down.

About four months earlier, I received a call from our partners at Target. To celebrate Black History Month in February and Women's History Month in March, the retailer was creating a bunch of content for a series they were calling "Founders We Believe In," in which they would highlight founders of color for various brands that they carried in store. They didn't share much else, but asked if I would be interested in being featured. I didn't need more information than "Target" and "content" to know that I wanted to do it. If Target wanted to call out Honey Pot, that would help sales and get us exposure. What else did I need to know? When a chance to help my company comes my way, I say yes. That said, I've learned not to assign too many expectations to even the most promising opportunities. One thing that fundraising taught me was that even when you have high expectations, and all the signs point to a positive outcome, it doesn't always go the way you hope. And also, on the flip side, expectations can be limiting. If I expect a product to sell a thousand units, I might stop pushing that product once we hit that goal. But what if that product was actually destined to sell a hundred thousand units? Now I've done myself and my business a disservice. You don't want to undermine your success by settling for less because your expectations were out of whack. These days, I'm grateful when any invitation comes my way. I say yes (most of the time), but I don't zero in on any specific result. I try to not expect anything and instead just show up and be myself and hopefully be surprised when something dope happens. That's the way I run my life.

It turns out, there's an unexpected downside to this seemingly nonchalant approach: trying to protect yourself from expectations can sometimes cut you off from information.

When the "Founders We Believe In" request came in, I didn't ask too many questions because I didn't want to get my hopes up about anything. In retrospect, I wonder if maybe I didn't ask enough questions! I just said, *OK, cool, let's do it.* My understanding was that Target was filming some sort of social media content, and that I'd be one of a bunch of founders featured. Imagine my surprise when they called again, only a few days before I was headed to their Minneapolis headquarters, and asked me if Simon and my mom could come, too. "You want to fly them to Minnesota for some social media footage?" I asked. "That seems unusual."

"Bea, this is going to be a major commercial," they said. "It will have a big budget and run on TV stations across the country."

That was new information.

Not only were we about to be featured in a nationally televised commercial, but I found out in that call that we were the only company getting that level of coverage. A few others did indeed get social media content, but it felt like Target was putting a lot of stock in Honey Pot, and giving us a pretty major vote of confidence. As a start-up business owner, this was a dream.

My mom, Simon, and I landed in Minneapolis on a Sunday afternoon in December. It was below zero outside and snowing and there was a sheet of ice on the ground. Anyone who has been to Minnesota in the middle of December knows the kind of cold I'm talking about—it's not your average winter weather.

It gets into your bones. And yet, despite the chill in the air and the giant amorphous winter coats we wore just to get from our car to the front door of the studio, those couple days were some of the most glamorous of my life up to that point. Target had partnered with a studio and put us up in a nice hotel. We woke up at 4 a.m. to get hair and makeup done and get dressed by a stylist. It was such a beautiful experience, and the energy around it was really positive. I had never done anything at that level, and Honey Pot could never have afforded to do something at that scale on our own. The whole shoot blew my mind, because nothing of that magnitude had ever happened to our business.

It was a two-day shoot. They filmed me and Simon and my mom at a Target store looking at our products on an end cap and in meetings with some of our Target partners, but they also interviewed me at length. That was going to be most of the commercial—me talking about the partnership with Target but also about the company in general. For that part, a producer sat me down and asked me what felt like a million questions. It was just a conversation, and I gave honest answers. One of the questions they asked was *Why is it so important to you, as an entrepreneur and the founder of Honey Pot, for your company to be successful?*

Under normal circumstances, my focus is on my company being human above all else. As human beings, we are more the same than we are different. We all have mouths and noses and fingers and toes. We all have similar desires for love and affection and relationships and success. I don't spend a lot of time focused on race, because I know race is a construct. It's not real. It's something that was created to keep people in order. But I'm also aware that in this culture and this society, I am not just considered a human, I am considered an African-American human. I am seen as a Black woman, and that is beautiful, but there is a lot of work that has been done to keep me as a Black woman and all humans with black skin or skin of color in a certain box. That is absolutely one of the reasons why venture capitalists and private equity firms only invest in a tiny percentage of Black women, and one of the reasons why of all the thousands of businesses that are traded on the stock market, only six (at least at the time of this writing) are Black-owned, and only one of those is led by a woman. It certainly doesn't have anything to do with any innate differences in business ability. It's not like white people are born with a better business sense. For that reason, it's important to me that other humans who look like me, and who have been put in the same box as me, understand that it's possible to achieve success and to aspire to big things and realize their dreams. It's also important to me that investors see the success of a Black-woman-led company. I was never told outright that any firm wasn't investing in Honey Pot because of race, but if I could help future Black founders have a slightly easier time than I did, that was valuable to me.

When that producer asked me why it was important that Honey Pot be a success, I explained that I want my company to be a case study for those who come after us. I want to be proof that it makes sense to invest in Black women. I want to help change the narrative—to say, *Look what we can do with our businesses when we are given opportunities.*

In the interview I said exactly that. Well, not exactly. "The reason why it's so important for Honey Pot to do well is so the next Black girl that comes up with a great idea, she could have a better opportunity," I said. "That means a lot to me."

The producer I spoke with probably asked me forty questions that day. We sat there for hours and hours, and he asked me my thoughts on any number of topics and I shared them honestly. We had a long and thoughtful conversation, and he could have used any quote I gave him, but my quote about inspiring Black girls is the one he chose. And that was fine by me. I thought it was powerful.

The commercial launched during the Super Bowl. The fucking Super Bowl! If you are going to have your company featured in only one commercial airing at only one time, the Super Bowl is it. I feel forever in Target's debt for that. I know they picked our company for a number of strategic reasons—we were one of the fastest-growing business of color at the time, we had powerful social media, we had a devoted customer base, and we had a great relationship with Target. They didn't just do it to be kind, but still, seeing myself on television during the Super Bowl felt like they had set us up for the long haul.

I didn't have many emotions around the commercial other than gratitude. It was a thirty-second spot, and it seemed pretty innocuous to me. The final shot of the ad was one of me and Simon and my mom, arms around each other, looking at our products in a Target store. That definitely felt poignant. After everything we'd all been through together, to be celebrated and featured on a national stage was meaningful.

And then, four weeks later, I started getting those "just checking in" texts. I'm not really a social media person—I maintain a profile because I'm the face of my company, but I don't spend a ton of time scrolling—but once I logged in, I saw there was a showdown happening in the comments section of our Instagram page.

It turned out, a group of women had latched onto my quote about Black girls and incited a major backlash against the ad, the company, and me. Their claim? That by calling out Black girls specifically, and my hope that they will have better opportunities in the future, I was being racist toward white people.

I don't know who it was that first took issue with the ad, but those who did rallied some of their friends, and these people launched a whole conversation about it online, calling the ad racist. They started a Trustpilot page where they flooded Honey Pot with negative reviews. Trustpilot is a company review website—it's like Glassdoor but for consumers—and in early March, over the course of two days, our company got eighteen thousand Trustpilot reviews. Eighteen thousand! In two days! Many of which were one-star, and the vast majority of which were clearly from people who'd never actually tried the products. The reviews included comments like "Boycott The Honey Pot Company, and Target. RACIST. White people hating comments not going to be tolerated," and "Black girls are empowered using this product . . . I guess white girls aren't. I'll be letting Target know about this racist company." Or this one, my personal favorite: "Their pads make me smell like Newport cigarettes." I mean, what?

To be clear, I didn't say in that ad, and have never said, that our products are only for Black humans. I simply said that one reason our success was important to me was so that Black girls can see themselves represented in business. The argument, from the many folks who decided to crusade against us, was that our company should be for all humans, not just Black ones. Which it is! But the reality is, all humans are not going to face the same disparities that I did. But other Black girls will. Those are just facts. And this producer asked *me*. He wanted *my* answer, and I told him my truth. I know the stats. I know what it's like to raise money as a Black woman in America. I know what it's like to be the underdog and to be put in a box that has nothing to do with who you are and everything to do with how others have decided you are, or how they want to see you. I'd love to live in a world where we don't have to talk about race and sex and all these constructions that only serve to hold certain groups down, but that's not where we are just yet. I love being a Black woman in business, but we have gone through it. Honey Pot's success is important to me for a number of reasons, and creating a path for Black businesswomen who come after me is absolutely one of them. Even if this ad hadn't been for Black History Month, I would have said the same thing. I'm grateful that we have Black History Month, but I also think it's weird that we have Black History Month—it should be Black History Year, just as all the other histories are year-long affairs.

I wish I could say I was incensed or even shocked by the crusade against our ad, but I've been a Black person in America for more than forty years. In other words, none of it surprised me. In fact, I didn't feel any sort of way about what was happening other than a real desire for it to pass. I wasn't about to put out a statement or try to defend what I said, because engaging with trolls is not the way. When you are dealing with trolls or even bots, you are dealing with people who don't have your best interests at heart. These were people who clearly had never tried our product. They had an agenda and had already made their decisions about our company, and it was not for me to make them feel differently. I'm not going to spend my time trying to convince racist people not to be racist. They have to come to that on their own, and it's not my responsibility as a human on this planet to control how other people think. If someone truly felt so bad about what I said that they were going to create a smear campaign and try to drag my company through the mud? Well, I guess they're going to do that. Honey Pot can't operate out of fear. I was thoughtful about what I said and how I said it, and I didn't have any regrets. My words were by no means intended to be disrespectful to anyone else, and I stood by them.

Luckily, my customers did too. One particular customer saw what was happening and got on social media and started posting her own campaign to rally our community around us. Our supporters became just as vocal as our haters—they started flooding Trustpilot with five-star ratings and posting positive comments, but they also started buying up our products and clearing them out of the stores. They supported us with their dollars, which is major.

The backlash eventually got to the point that Trustpilot had to turn off the review function for our company's page while its content integrity team investigated the onslaught of reviews, "some of which violate Trustpilot's guidelines," they said. Target issued a statement of support for our partnership, too. "Target has a longstanding commitment to empowering and investing in diverse suppliers that create a broad variety of products for our guests," they said. "We're proud to work with Bea Dixon and The Honey Pot team to highlight Bea's journey to build her brand and bring her products to Target."

The media also took notice. I ended up giving a huge number of interviews, both in publications like *BuzzFeed* and *Teen Vogue* and *Forbes*, and on CNBC and TV shows like *The Dr. Oz Show* and *The Real*. Other than in the commercial, this was the first time I was out there representing our brand as Bea, the woman and cofounder. I should have been nervous, but I didn't even have time for nerves because I was moving at such a fast clip. I wasn't thinking, I was just doing. On *The Real*, they asked me what I thought the issue was—what was upsetting people so much. "I give those people grace; I don't know what their situation is or what they've been through," I said. "But the facts still stand, and if I had to change [what I said] I wouldn't . . . The fact is there is a huge disparity when it comes to Black women raising capital, and we can't look past that." In each of those appearances I was able to speak directly to why I said what I said in the commercial, but I was also able to express my gratitude for the customers who rallied around us, because if I had any takeaway from the experience, that was it. I even had gratitude for the haters, both because the entire episode led to a significant increase in sales, but also because it served as a reminder that our community—as in the people who actually use and engage with Honey Pot—is bound by support and positivity. I was so moved by the energy and the connection that poured out of the people who built our brand, and had been with us since the beginning. As a show of support, they invested even more of their hard-earned dollars in our products and got their friends to do the same.

I cannot overstate how powerful it is when customers come together to spend their money and support a product on the shelves. My customers are the single most important piece of our business. No one is going to invest big money in your company if your customers aren't willing to invest their dollars in your product. Customers are the ones who create the reason for a company to seek funding in the first place. But it's not just the customers that buy your products that matter. Honey Pot has supporters who are invested in the success of our brand even if, for example, they can't afford our products or they simply choose not to use them. That's totally fine. People who support us and help propel our success, in whatever way they can, they matter. And this whole episode reminded me that

that's the relationship we need to always foster. Our customers even helped us manage the social media backlash—they were jumping in and defending us against the racist commenters. That's such a testament to the humans that Honey Pot serves. They were ready. There was so much kindness and care and love and unity from our supporters that I get emotional just writing about it. My positive feelings of gratitude and honor and appreciation were so much bigger than any negative feelings that the trolls really lost out on this one.

Before this moment, I hadn't given much thought to what it meant to lead a company. I was thinking about the hustle, and the freedom, but I didn't focus on the part where I had to guide other people or establish company norms or be the face of the brand. In 2020, in large part due to this controversy, Honey Pot saw a huge amount of growth, and so we decided to invest in building our team. We grew from a small group of about ten people to a company of about thirty employees. The pandemic circumstances of that year dictated that we hire remote positions, but that worked out perfectly for us, because I always wanted to be a work-from-anywhere company. We have a beautiful office space in Atlanta, and some people work from there, but I always knew that what mattered was to build a team of the best humans for the job, no matter where they lived. I don't care if you reside in Atlanta or Alaska—if you are aligned with our mission and show the potential to positively affect our business and culture and customers, we want you on our team.

And yet, no matter how amazing your team, building a business in these modern times means that some individual needs to publicly represent your business. Companies didn't always require having a "face" to the brand. Before social media, a start-up company could roll out a product and people didn't pay much attention to who was behind it. The product usually stood for itself. I'm not sure if that was a good thing or not—having a public persona behind a business ensures some level of accountability, and it keeps a company human. I want people to know that Honey Pot is a company of humans serving humans. I want our customers to know my story—to know that these products I'm suggesting they use on their vaginas, I used them (and still use them) on mine. I would never ask someone to put anything in their body that I wouldn't use myself, and that's an important piece of our brand narrative. But that kind of exposure also serves someone up on a silver platter when anyone out there—customer or not—has a complaint about the company. Social media is a breeding ground for online trolls, and for viral moments. It fans the flames of any tiny fire, so a moment that could have come and gone without doing much damage can suddenly turn into a blaze of chaos.

Our Target controversy, if you can even call it that, was Honey Pot's first viral moment as a company. Our website and social media accounts got hundreds of millions of views. We'd never had attention like that before, and we'd certainly never been the topic of online chatter. In addition to shining a light on our loyal and steadfast customer base, it also taught me that the business, and the brand, is resilient. It can take a punch, and that's important. If you are trying to build and grow a company in today's cancel-culture climate, you need to know that you can withstand a little drama, because any company with enough eyes on it will come under fire eventually, even if they've done nothing wrong. It's the nature of the world we live in, and if you crumble at the first bout of negative press, or you haven't built a customer base that will stand behind you in hard times, then your brand might not be around very long. In some ways, just the fact that we were *able* to go viral was exciting, because it felt like a sign that our work was resonating, and that people were paying attention. If all press is good press, then there we were, basking in the attention, happy to get our fifteen minutes of fame.

If nothing else, the Target commercial crisis was a learning opportunity. Because where there is one viral moment, there will be another, and when our next one came, I was just a bit more ready.

Eventually, we made it through the drama of our Target ad. Keep in mind that all that fanfare happened in early March of 2020. The two days of Trustpilot reviews were on March 1 and 2. A couple weeks later a global pandemic took center stage, and then no one was talking about our racist trolls, they were talking about whether they could leave the house or go to the office or see their friends. Covid posed additional difficulties for us, on top of the already quite difficult global health crisis, because just as we were getting inundated with those orders in support of our business, global supply chain logistics were getting extra complicated, and fulfilling orders became nearly impossible. But, like I said, eventually our story became yesterday's news and we moved forward as a company.

A couple years later, in 2022, we were an even bigger company. We had more products and more employees and we were being sold in more stores. But supply chain issues still existed in the wake of Covid and we were having trouble getting some of our ingredients in stock, and even more trouble keeping others in stock. Also, our brand had gone global, but one of our ingredients—colloidal silver—was not allowed in certain countries. Colloidal silver is a solution of tiny silver particles in liquid that's good for the skin, but it also helps to preserve the formulation of the product and make it last longer. It's a great ingredient, but different countries have different regulations, and in some countries it's classified as a drug. It's not scalable, and we wanted to be available in as many places as possible. Colloidal silver wasn't indispensable to our product, so we decided to go back and reformulate our washes. We changed our preservative system and (I feel particularly strongly about this point) we made it better.

Brands like ours make changes to their formulas all the time. Most of the time, customers don't really care. As long as they're still getting the same quality product, a formulation change doesn't make much of a splash. In this instance, our team didn't call attention to the alteration, not because we were trying to bury it but because we were still a relatively young brand doing a million things at once, so while we listed all the ingredients properly on our packaging, we didn't make any sort of announcement to say *hey, our formulation has evolved.* And because we were doing more robust clinical trials, we dialed down the language on our packaging. Instead of "gynecologist approved" we said "dermatologist approved."

Soon after we rolled out our reformulation, some of our customers started posting angry videos on TikTok and long captions on Instagram. They questioned us for making changes without publicly announcing them. They worried the washes were no longer gynecologist approved or pH balanced (they were). They claimed the new ingredients were harmful (they weren't). One popular TikTok video implied that, as a company, we could no longer be trusted. Plus, rumors started circulating that we had sold the company (we hadn't) and thus were no longer Black-owned (we were). Suddenly there were extensive Twitter threads between customers and chemists and all different types of so-called "experts" weighing in and making assumptions about choices we'd made as a company. The phrase "selling out" was used a lot. The conversation snowballed, as these things do, and the story went viral. It grew so big that I was eventually receiving actual death threats online. Death threats! Anytime something goes viral, people create narratives, and there's very little time spent trying to assess if these stories are true or false. This was a prime example of how quickly misinformation spreads in today's digital environment.

The major difference between this episode and the commotion around the Target ad was that the negativity was now coming from our customer base. The first time around, we got slammed, but it was primarily by individuals who had never used Honey Pot. But after the reformulation, the negativity came from people who had until then been loyal and passionate customers, and that was incredibly hard for me. It affected me differently. If I was solid as a rock during the Target fiasco, this time I was really hurting, emotionally and physically. Strangers were putting words in my mouth, and I felt helpless. Having my customers question my integrity and send all this negative energy toward me and my company was draining. In the immediate aftermath, I could hardly get out of bed in the morning, knowing I would face another day of vitriol. When I did get out of bed, I was plagued with lower back and shoulder pain. Usually being an empath works in my favor, but here it meant I was absorbing all the negativity coming our way and carrying it in my body. And I did that on purpose, because it felt better that I bore the brunt of it than the people who worked with me. I was trying to protect them—that felt like my job as the leader—but it weighed me down. I would burst into tears during company calls. I went on a women's business retreat that I'd scheduled long before this controversy broke out, and while I was there I would be in conversation with another businesswoman and suddenly burst into tears. Mid-conversation! But people were using words like "poison" to describe our products, which is antithetical to everything we stand for as a company, and that affected me deeply. I am the CEO and chief innovation officer of this brand, and I would never *ever* make a product for human consumption that I didn't think was beautiful and healing above all else. To be accused of doing something intentionally harmful when my true intention has always been the complete opposite of that . . . it was devastating.

Of course, I wasn't the only individual affected by this crisis. It was torture on our team. The humans who work in our social media and customer service departments were steeped in negative comments all day. When they're sitting anonymously behind a screen, people will say extreme or nasty things that they would never say to another human being in person. The angry folks online were treating Honey Pot like we were a faceless business, but we are a company made up of individuals who care about the work we do. Every single mean and demeaning comment was being read by someone who had feelings and a life. They had woken up that day with a determination to put good work into the world, and now they were fending off anger they didn't deserve. The employees at Honey Pot give it everything they have and take a lot of pride in their work. They believe in the mission. And a lot of them are young people who really care a lot about social media, and now they were being inundated with negativity in a place that had previously felt safe. On top of that, they were working twelve- to fourteen-hour shifts to manage our accounts and field the inquiries and comments that were pouring in. They were working through weekends, sometimes for fourteen days straight, and none of that was in their job description. Plus, they were working from home! Because we're mostly remote, we didn't have the opportunity to gather around the water cooler and support each other with the in-person camaraderie that can help in these situations. My team was exhausted and burnt out. No one ever threatened to quit, but I do think some individuals started questioning themselves and their work product, and for me that was the most heartbreaking of all. At first, I didn't know how to give them the tools they needed. I wanted to motivate them but wasn't sure how.

On company Zooms, which were happening multiple times a week since we were in crisis mode, I would encourage the team to not absorb the bad energy, but that's easier said than done. I would encourage them to take time to themselves, but that was difficult given how much work they had piling up. In the days immediately following this controversy, we'd decided as a team that we would respond to the comments, because we wanted to correct any misinformation. But eventually I decided it wasn't worth it—I couldn't keep asking my employees to interact with people who weren't being kind or treating them with respect. We shut down the comments on our posts. We weren't going to change people's minds on that individual level, and if we couldn't have an open and productive conversation with our users, I was no longer willing to subject our team members to that level of negativity.

We also offered additional resources for our employees that we hoped, in that moment and in the future, would make their lives a little bit easier. We enlisted a life coach that our employees could talk to about work-life balance, and career counselors who could help them set and implement goals for growth within the company. We sent everyone $20 for Uber Eats so we could buy them lunch even if we couldn't eat together. If they worked over a weekend, we gave them days off during the week so they could get some rest. We added mental health days in addition to sick days. And since it was an all-hands-on-deck situation, we asked people in other departments to jump in and help so it wasn't the same group of people managing the onslaught day in and day out. Above all else, we were honest about what had happened and what we were doing to address it, because it feels crappy as an employee when you are working around the clock but haven't been trusted with the truth of what's going on.

> I deeply believe in transparency, and we have such a genuine relationship with our customers—so much so that they notice a change in an ingredient—that I knew I had to address the situation directly.

I am always willing to accept responsibility when I make a misstep. In the case of our reformulation, we should have been more transparent and flagged the change as soon as we made it to get ahead of any backlash. It never occurred to me that anyone would react this strongly to the change, or care at even close to the levels that it turned out they did. That was my mistake. We ended up posting an extensive explanation on our social accounts in the hopes of clearing up any confusion, but I also filmed and posted a video explaining what happened in my own words. It was the exact opposite of what our public relations firm told us to do. We had a PR firm that we'd worked with in the past, and we solicited additional advice for this particular crisis situation. "Let it pass," the PR folks told me when I asked for advice on how to proceed. "Responding to negative comments gives a controversy legs—we want this to go away." It's PR 101, they said. You don't engage with or argue with the customer when they are angry. But my gut was telling me that wasn't the right approach this time, and I listen to my gut. These people knew PR, but I knew the Honey Pot community. I deeply believe in transparency, and we have such a genuine relationship with our customers—so much so that they notice a change in an ingredient—that I knew I had to address the situation directly. Everyone in a relationship deserves a say in some form or fashion. We couldn't just hope and pray it would pass, because it wouldn't. People wanted answers. I wanted to provide them. I wanted those people to understand what we did and why we did it. A little information can go a long way, and I had nothing to hide. I knew that the changes we made were actually to the brand's and the customer's benefit, and so I said as much. I explained that the evolution of our wash formulation increased the shelf life of the product without changing the quality. I also owned up to where we fell short. But then, at the same time, I had to ask my customers to live up to the standards to which they were holding me and my team. Why was I getting death threats because I changed a preservative? That's not OK! Ultimately, all I could do was be open and honest with our community, and I'm happy we took that approach, because it helped us retain some customers.

As employees, our value system became: If we can stand behind what we do and acknowledge when we make a misstep, then we've lived up to our responsibility. Building any big venture involves a learning curve, and this was ours. We should have been more communicative, and yet again, there was so much we learned from what was a really hard and sometimes ugly experience. For one, I realized we were even more important to our customers than I knew. That's a blessing—customers who care are what keep a company in business. That reminder inspired us to be even more intentional about what we say and how we say it, which has only improved our practices. Now, anytime we are thinking about making a change, that consideration is partnered with the question *How will we communicate this change to our customers early, so that by the time it actually goes into effect, they know about it and are comfortable with it?* We've also begun gathering even more customer data on any decision we're considering. We don't just decide we're going to do something and do it, we say, *Hey, we're maybe going to do this, let's go to our longest-standing customers and see what they think.* We have a membership program, The Hive, and we ask those members about their priorities. We might post something on social asking for feedback. We learned from those viral moments that we need to be in conversation with the people we serve and bring them on the journey. We're even more transparent now, because we're always thinking about how we can go above and beyond to serve the people who support our brand.

As much as this moment reminded me to take responsibility when I can, it also reminded me that I can't take responsibility for everything. I understand that these days there is a knee-jerk cynicism toward leaders in every field. And I understand why. Customers across industries have been lied to and hoodwinked in so many ways, of course they automatically assume a company has negative intent. If you were in a long-term relationship and then were hurt by that person, when you meet someone new, even if they want to do right by you, it's harder to trust. Being in a relationship with a business is similar. If you've been a consumer of a company that turned out to be treating their customers poorly—misrepresenting products or including harmful ingredients, for example—of course you will be more skeptical moving forward. You may assume that no matter what the next company does, they are only concerned with the bottom line. And, at the same time, you might expect them to get everything right the first time, with no exceptions. When they don't, you're ready to pounce, because you've been burned before. But it's a lot to expect of anybody. And that's what I am. A human being, a body, made of skin and bone and tissue. If thousands of clients start spewing hatred, I am going to have a reaction. Words are a form of energy, and we all should be careful with them. I have to imagine that most business owners feel the same way I do. At least the business owners of companies that are a similar size to Honey Pot. Customers see us in stores like CVS or Target and assume we must be made up of thousands of employees, so that no single person will be affected if the mob comes for us. But Honey Pot still has fewer than one hundred employees. That's the case for most businesses like us—ones that are successful but not yet part of huge conglomerates. Customers may view us as "just a business," but when you've built something from nothing, it means you've put so much energy and life force into it that there's no way it isn't personal.

If someone wants to spout negativity, I can't stop them. And we at Honey Pot can't serve everyone, no matter how hard we try. While we always knew that intellectually, watching people get on the internet and make wild claims just reminded me that I'm not in control of other people. I can't dictate how they think or how they act and what they say, even if the things they say are straight-up false, or even blatantly racist. It's not OK for people to spew hatred and lies, but it's also their prerogative to spew hatred and lies. I had to learn not to internalize those comments, but it wasn't easy. I knew the difficulty of this one was going to create a trauma bubble for our team at Honey Pot, and as the leader of the company I felt a responsibility to manage that and protect the emotional and physical health of my employees. But I had to protect myself as well. I've said it here already, but I'm an intuitive. I'm an empath. A lot of people claim that title nowadays because it's the thing to say, but it's very real for me. Extremely public or viral moments can be especially hard for me for that reason, because I can feel all the energy that is pointed in my direction. I might cry or have back pain or need a nap where another person would be fine. In this case, there were millions of people paying attention to these controversies, and that's a lot of energy being funneled in one person's direction. Not all of it was negative, but enough of it was, and that was hard.

Clearly, being in the public eye hasn't been easy for me. I think that surprises people sometimes, because of the way I talk and how authentically I show up. I might call my company "the vagina company" or make a joke to break the ice at a conference, and because of that, people think I'm totally at ease. And it's true that, most of the time, I don't get especially nervous—but that doesn't mean I enjoy the spotlight. Outward attention is not why I got into this business. I got into it to help liberate and heal other humans, and to get my bread and support my family and do the work that will retire me. The attention piece just happened. It wasn't a strategic decision. If someone at work had said, *Hey, Bea, we want you to be the face of the company*, that would have felt really weird. But that's not how it went down at all. If I was going to share the story of how Honey Pot came to be, I had to embrace the fact that my face and my personality would be embedded into the brand. I had to be willing to do what was necessary to get our story and our mission across. I took that on because this is what I was born to do.

Honey Pot is my life's work, so while I'm grateful for the attention, it's not my focus or my motivation. If it were up to me, I would be sitting in the corner minding my business, doing my job, drinking my water, spending time with my family and friends, traveling and enjoying my life. But I don't take it lightly that I have been given this opportunity. The fact that the ailments I have experienced with my own body have created a movement that others can participate in and experience in their own bodies and even use to heal from their own traumas—that is some deeply connected shit. It makes all my experiences feel bigger than just me, which takes me out of my own head and my own suffering, even when things feel extraordinarily complicated or painful or just plain difficult.

Still, even when I can see the deeper meaning, it doesn't make the hard times less hard. And being the leader of a company as well as its public face—which means I'm in the ads and the website photography, but I'm also the spokesperson answering media inquiries and the representative on panels and the person delivering the messages to customers when things go wrong—it's taxing. It can wear on a person. It's hard to give so much of yourself. Maybe one day I'll learn to compartmentalize or go through the motions of speaking on behalf of the company without investing my heart and soul into those moments, but I'm not there yet. I'm not sure that's how I'll ever want to live. Right now, when I'm on, I'm on. I'm never reciting a speech someone wrote for me or saying words I don't connect to, because I don't know how to do that. I don't know how to show up with a different voice depending on the audience I'm speaking to. I'm not trying, I'm just doing, and I don't know how to be anything less than transparent. I know we celebrate authenticity and transparency above all else these days, but would it be easier if I could just put on a mask to present to the world when necessary? Probably. But at the same time I truly believe Honey Pot wouldn't have gotten to where we are today—and powered through these public storms—if I was a corporate robot. Our customers are simply smarter than that, which is one of the many reasons why I love and appreciate them.

Of course, being a leader is as much an internal job as an external one. As much as our customers are always watching, so are the Honey Pot employees.

If I'm in a company meeting and I seem super stressed or in a sad mood, that energy is going to rub off on the rest of our team. I believe wholeheartedly that the employees of Honey Pot work *with* me not *for* me, but I'm not blind to the fact that I sit at the top of the org chart. I know that I set the tone for the company culture, and even sometimes for the mood of the day. I know that if I appear out of sorts, it can raise questions like: *Why is she upset? Is something going on with the business? Should we be worried?* Also, when shit gets complicated, your team will turn to you to make the hard decisions. That's a powerful position to be in, but it also means you need to know how to handle it if your decision isn't the right one. This, for me, has been the key to effective leadership. I pride myself on having a pretty good sense of what Honey Pot needs at any given time or what might be the best next move for our brand.

That said, no matter who you are or how much experience you have, one person cannot do everything for a company. Even in the earliest days of Honey Pot, I had Simon's partnership, and fairly quickly we added incredible humans to the team. As a company grows, its needs grow too. Once you have employees, for example, you need to have payroll and HR. You have to establish the culture you want to uphold, and the values you want to instill. Hiring employees is a huge responsibility—you are pretty much saying, *Come work with me and I am going to make sure you can feed your family and pay your bills and have a car and a roof over your head.* That's a major promise you're making to someone, and no matter how experienced a leader you are, one person cannot necessarily ensure a good experience for all employees while also paying attention to production and finances and marketing. One major point of pride for me as the leader of Honey Pot is that I know what I'm good at and I'm aware that I don't know what I don't know. I have surrounded myself with people who are smarter than me and people whose skillsets complement mine, and that's very important. I don't pretend to have a handle on everything when it comes to business. I understand a lot more now than I did when my grandmother came to me in a dream, that's for sure, because real-world experience is the best teacher. But when I find myself working too much in an area of the business I don't fully understand, I can quickly recognize that I need to bring someone in who knows how to do certain things better than I do, or who can at least help alongside me. A lot of company leadership is innate—you learn as you go and you figure it out on the fly. But sometimes you don't want to figure it out and you don't have time to learn it, or you can tell you'll never understand something the way someone who went to school and graduated with a business degree and has years of hands-on experience will. Our current president and CFO was the right person for her role because she had corporate experience that I will never have. She had been a VP or CFO at several Fortune 500 companies, and she has done this work for a very long time. Whereas I have an innate connection to our mission and spirit, she brings decades of know-how. Our knowledge bases complement each other, and together we cover more ground. That matters, especially now, because mistakes, while they will happen, are more expensive once your company is bigger and more eyes are on you. Not only do they cost your company more

> I truly believe Honey Pot wouldn't have gotten to where we are today—and powered through these public storms—if I was a corporate robot. Our customers are simply smarter than that, which is one of the many reasons why I love and appreciate them.

money to fix, but they affect more people, both employees and customers. If you are going to ask your employees—human beings with full lives—to come and work with you and essentially build out your dream, you have to be able to take care of them properly. And if you are going to ask human beings in the world to take money out of their wallets to spend on your product, you best be serving their well-being at all times.

Today, my measure of success as a leader is not how often I get everything right, but how swiftly I react when things go wrong. What's important is that you focus on solutions over problems. If I can see when something is not working and can extract the poison real quick without a lot of panic, that to me is successful leadership. It might be that someone we hired is not the right fit, or a product line isn't resonating, or a partner we've decided to work with isn't jelling. The ability to pay attention and identify those hiccups early so that you can act on them immediately, before your whole company is riled up, is what I consider the mark of a great leader. I like to ask myself and my team: *What did we learn? What do we have to fix?* I often say it's important to fail fast, but what I mean, really, is that you act fast in the face of the failures. You have to be willing to see the failure and say, *Oops, OK, what's the next move?* So, for example, if you have a manufacturer that's not working out, failing fast is not merely realizing that this

> You have to establish the culture you want to uphold, and the values you want to instill.

is a bad fit and quickly getting out of it. Failing fast is having another manufacturer on deck, one that you can immediately vet and audit. It's making sure, in a timely manner, that they'll make your product better or faster or cleaner. You need to visit their plant, and you should have more than one of these options lined up. An option A and an option B and an option C. You need to back up your backup because any number of things can go wrong at any time, and you want to stay a step ahead.

> Today, my measure of success as a leader is not how often I get everything right, but how swiftly I react when things go wrong. What's important is that you focus on solutions over problems.

There will be another viral moment. Another hot seat. Another controversy. At least, there will be if we're lucky, because it will mean Honey Pot is still surviving and thriving. Each public crisis that Honey Pot faced helped write and revise the playbook we will rely on when we next experience a controversy. With the Target ad, we learned how much we meant to our customers. The way they showed up for us and defended us was really beautiful. After our formulation change, we learned that our customers are deeply paying attention, and also that they can turn on us. The relationship with a customer is delicate, so it needs to be cared for delicately. We learned that transparency is important but so is trusting our instincts. And each of these moments gave me additional strength as a leader too, because that which is hard makes us stronger. When the next controversy happens, we'll learn and grow from that one too, because I believe we will be here for a very long time. Right now, my playbook for these moments is clear: Respect myself, but also respect my customer. Don't beat myself up, but if I did something wrong, say it. Then, help people understand what we'll do differently next time. Be solution-oriented, but also know my truth. What do I mean by that? Well, other people will come up with their own truths. People on Instagram and TikTok will believe the story that they've concocted. The media will believe their own version. Our competitors will believe another. Mostly likely, none of these versions will align with the actual truth. We could do our damnedest to get our version—the real story—out there, and sometimes that will work, but other times (most times) it won't. We can only control so much, and a media narrative usually takes on a life of its own. And there may be times when we don't even want to share our truth—when we want to keep the truth for ourselves and for the people who need to know. But the playbook is always iterating, because mistakes are where you learn the most. When you touch something and burn your finger, you aren't going to touch that thing again.

So when I find myself wanting to stay in bed all day because articles about our company are getting the facts wrong, I remind myself to breathe. *Bea, you're fucking tripping*, I say. *This is the media, and they are always going to get shit wrong.* Just reminding myself of that helps. People love tea. They will click on any link to get it, and clicks equal cash. All of which to say, the story might be about me, but it's not really *about* me. It's about profit and generating attention.

Once I know my truth, I can live in it, and when I can live in it, I can make a conscious choice about how to react. If I get out of my mind and into my body and the present moment and a place that is positive, I can make better, more sensible choices. As important as it was for Honey Pot to choose to speak up and explain ourselves when anger was being thrown our way, I would never categorically recommend that for another company. You have to know what's right for you and your brand. Take care of yourself, because if you don't, just one moment of public scrutiny can take you out. It can screw with your head. I know this because I almost got there myself. I would have been served better by staying off the emotional roller coaster altogether. It's not the exciting thrill ride it seems.

If you ever find yourself in situations like these, I hope you will take care of yourself. But also, take care of your team. Make sure they know they're cared for and appreciated. When you are the face of a company it can feel like all the heat is coming at you, but the people who have your business name on their LinkedIn profile, who have publicly pledged to support you and your dream, they are feeling the pressure and the negativity just as strongly. They are answering for you, maybe even defending you, even if you haven't done anything wrong.

At Honey Pot, one of our taglines is that we are "made by

humans with vaginas, for humans with vaginas." When people read that, they often put the emphasis on the word *vagina*, but to me the most important part is the word *human*. The customers we serve are humans—they are not just dollar signs—and that drives everything we do. But also, the people who make these products—me, my team—we are also humans. When public and heated controversies like these arise, I wonder if that's the one fact we all need to remember: Behind the businesses and the social handles and the skepticism and the defensiveness are just people trying to do their best work and put one foot in front of the other. They just want to be seen and understood. It's humanity 101.

Chapter Ten

A Cleanse for the Soul

In 2021, I took a trip to Tulum, Mexico, with a friend. I'd just recently gotten divorced and was in need of some serious healing. The trip was intended to be a relaxing escape—a way to unplug and begin to recover from what had been a tough couple of years. Obviously, the divorce had taken a lot out of me. I was exhausted and overwhelmed, and for a while I'd lived in fear of what I might have to give up in the split. It was a financial worry, because I'd been working hard to build something and didn't want that taken away from me. But it was also an emotional worry. One of the things that divorce takes from you is the dream you had for your life. When you marry someone, you plan to be with them forever. You think you are forging a beautiful partnership. Divorce strips a person of that dream, and you have to grieve that loss like a death. It wore on me. You could see it in my body—I could barely stand up straight, my face had dulled. I was tired and stressed out and maybe a little bit depressed, though I wouldn't have said that at the time.

My marriage wasn't the only relationship that had changed recently. While the growth of Honey Pot had been a blessing, I learned quickly that the more successful you get—and thus the more access and abundance you have—the more people ask of you. Friends, families, professional acquaintances . . . it seemed that everyone needed a favor, whether it was time or money, an introduction or advice. For a long time, saying no was hard for me. I'm a nice person. I'm not always attached to material goods, or even intangible ones. If I have a friend who is really struggling and I can help, why would I watch them struggle? If I have a whole piece of something and you're hungry, why wouldn't I give you half? I'm proud to be a giver in that way, but it makes it easy for people to take advantage of you. Whether it's cash or love or anything in between, I find that people are willing to take what's available to them.

I had traveled to Mexico to heal, but I was also there to recharge, because I was about to face a stretch of time at work that I knew would ask a lot of me. Honey Pot had been seeing a lot of growth and success, and Simon and our leadership team and I decided to get the company ready to start looking for a sale. That was the next stage of growing this business, but that endeavor—which, like asking for investments, involves tons of conferences and questions and close calls and rejections—would be taxing. It would wear on my body and my mind. It required constantly meeting with people, constantly selling myself, constantly being let down, and I knew from that past that it's a level of busy that, if you are crumbling in any way personally, will shut you down. I had to rid my body of the trauma of the last few years because what I was walking into would be a different sort of trauma. Even if it ultimately led to a good outcome, it was going to be a long and arduous process, and if I didn't go into it as healthy as possible, I was setting myself up for failure.

We were staying at Habitas, this really dope sustainable adults-only hotel in Tulum that is specifically focused on community empowerment, well-being, and spirituality. It was almost like glamping—the rooms were more like tents, with thatched roofs and canvas walls and outdoor rain showers. While I was staying there, I kept noticing this other woman, who I felt strangely drawn to. She was white and blonde, average height—she had the look that some might describe as "hippy"—and she just had this energy that was intense but also healing. I thought she was a guest at the hotel. One morning I arrived to breakfast alone and there she was again, sitting one table over.

"Hi," she said. "What brings you to Habitas?"

"I just needed to unplug and relax," I said. "It's so beautiful here. What about you? I feel like I see you everywhere."

"The hotel flew me in for the week," she said. "I'm a trauma healer."

Her name was Kirsty, and she began to tell me her story—she grew up in the Australian outback and had a pretty rustic upbringing with a lot of her own family trauma, but now she worked with the likes of Oprah, helping people dig into their history, confront hard truths, move past fear, and find spiritual fulfillment. She was clearly passionate about her work and talked about it with a lot of seriousness. To some people she probably seemed like a lot—later in the week, my friend mentioned how intense she was—but if you're a shaman and a healer, you're going to be intense. It's not the kind of work you mess around with. I appreciate that level of commitment.

Kirsty and I ended up sitting in that restaurant talking for over an hour. I told her about my work and my divorce. "I probably need to do some serious healing," I said, "but I'm not sure I can handle digging as deep as you're talking right now."

After that morning, Kirsty and I only spoke one or two more times that week, but we exchanged numbers. She told me to reach out when I was ready. She didn't pressure me at all, but she checked in from time to time after the trip. For a while, I was too overwhelmed to think about meeting with her. What I knew about Kirsty's work was that it was deep and difficult. In some of her most intense sessions, she took people back to the hardest moments of their lives. She warned me that to do the level of healing I needed, it would be emotional and raw and maybe even ugly. But on the other side would be beauty and fulfillment. I knew that reaching out to her again could offer a lot of positives, but also that I couldn't do it until I was good and ready. I couldn't be questioning why I was there, and I had to be willing to accept whatever might come up. It had to be an undeniable yes, because I was pretty sure we were going to uncover some gnarly stuff.

About seven months after that trip to Mexico, I decided it was time to shed the film of hurt and trauma and resentment that had been building on my spirit since . . . well, forever. Much of it was due to divorce, but I knew I was holding on to other hurts from my past, whether it was the abuse from my family member or the hard moments from my hustling days in Atlanta. And I knew there was probably some sticky residue from moments I wasn't even overtly conscious of.

I wanted to work with Kirsty specifically not only because she was clearly passionate and experienced, but also because the way we met felt like a sign. She came into my life at the exact moment that I needed to meet a medicine woman, so I called her up and told her it was time.

To start, we did a couple of counseling sessions over Zoom, marked mostly by breath work. She led me through a guided meditation and regression experience, in which she helped me access memories from my past. It left me feeling freer and lighter. There was much more work to be done, but even those short sessions with Kirsty gave me the confidence to believe I wouldn't always be haunted or held hostage by the hardest moments of my past. Healing was possible.

And so it was with Kirsty, about a year later, that I decided to do a mushroom ceremony. I had to work myself up to the idea, because I knew the experience might be a little bit scary. I really had no idea what it would entail, except that it would be an intense journey under the influence of a serious dose of psilocybin mushrooms. That alone can be intimidating. I'd done my share of recreational drugs, but this would not be that. Plus, Kirsty takes her work seriously. I knew that if I embarked on this journey, it would be much more than just a "go to Mexico and do some shrooms!" situation. There was no partying on the agenda, no fun trips. This would be serious.

Preparation for the mushroom ceremony began about a month in advance. I had to eat vegan, because I couldn't consume anything with consciousness. There was very little alcohol or weed allowed—no vices, pretty much, because Kirsty said I needed to go into the ceremony with a clear head.

In July 2022, I flew to Mexico City to meet with Kirsty and her sister, Ana, who was a light worker. She administers light therapy, bringing practitioners into a deep meditative state. From Mexico City, we traveled about two hours to Tepoztlán, a town known for UFO sightings and its wildly growing trees but also for its mystical and spiritual qualities. Legend has it that Tepoztlán is the birthplace of Quetzalcóatl, the feathered serpent god of Aztec culture. As soon as we arrived in Tepoztlán, we got a vegan lunch and then got right to work, starting with more breath work and regression therapy. This wasn't like your average yoga-class breath work. We were doing the breath of fire—rapid exhalations out the nose—but going so hard with it that I felt like I might pass out. Kirsty instructed me to close my eyes and think about my past and any people who had hurt me. She sat down close and faced me. "I want you to imagine that whoever is coming up for you right now, I am that person," she said. "Tell me what you want me to know. Let it all out—the anger or sadness or resentment or questions you've always wanted to unleash."

The names and faces of people I wanted to confront came to me easily. I'd come to this trip very ready, and had prepared by reflecting on moments I knew were still sitting with me. Also, a lot of my deepest hurt was very recent, which made it especially easy to access. I found myself quickly getting very angry, and not just telling Kirsty what I wanted these people to know, but screaming at her with rage. It was powerful—she helped me access anger that I didn't even know I had—and it was clear the next few days were going to be intense, vulnerable, and effective.

Next was the light work, the likes of which I'd never experienced. Ana uses something called a PandoraStar, a device that emits high-frequency LED lights, which eased me into various phases of meditation and consciousness. I saw all these beautiful colors—they came and went so quickly that I couldn't even distinguish one from the next—and they formed shapes and patterns that would swirl and transition and basically encompass my whole awareness. The lights helped ease me into a deep state of spiritual and emotional openness, which I would need for the mushroom ceremony to come.

The next day, Kirsty, Ana, and I went to my *temazcal*, a

ritual of spiritual and bodily renewal. The *temazcal* itself was a tiny hut—we crawled in and sat in a pit where we sweat out toxins, leaving our bodies cleansed and ready for the mushroom ceremony. The *temazcal* ritual was incredible, and if you'd told me after that ceremony that our work in Mexico was done, I would have said it had been a meaningful experience. And we hadn't even gotten to the main event yet. There was a medicine worker who led the *temazcal* ceremony, which was largely focused on connecting with my ancestors, and he chanted all these beautiful songs and prayers. We sat there for a few hours before returning once again to the light therapy. The care and love that went into the entire experience was truly incredible, but by the end of the second day, I was like an open wound. I was as raw and exposed and as receptive as I'd ever been in my life—mentally, emotionally, spiritually, and physically. And I was someone whose spirit had been pretty open in the first place. I'd done plenty of work to get it that way. But now I'd spent two days in ceremony, clearing out layers of scar tissue that had developed as a form of soul protection. I did all that to ensure there was no guard up when I took the medicine and got into the real work.

When I woke up the next day, the third day, it was time to take the medicine. I'd already felt like I'd had a pretty crazy couple of days, but this was the moment I had come to this sacred space for. And pretty much the moment you're in it, you're *in it*. As much as I may have thought I knew what was coming, it turns out I had no fucking idea. Zero. This is the kind of thing you simply can't imagine or anticipate until you're in it. And it's better that way. Honestly, I'm not sure if I would have signed up if I'd had any sense of what was coming.

As we began, we entered a cave. Kirsty gave me the medicine—a hero's dose of psilocybin mushrooms—and I remember her telling me that as soon as I felt it working, I had to tell her. She and Ana took mushrooms with me, but a much smaller dose. Because my spirit was so wide open—thanks to the month of prep and the past two days of intense work—I felt the mushrooms almost immediately. At this point, we went inside the house where we were staying, then they blindfolded me in order to help me go inward and to protect me from over-stimulation. Next, they started singing and chanting. It sounds scary, I know, and it was, in its way.

It's hard to describe the next nine hours of my life. It was otherworldly. I was transported to a place that was . . . not here. I don't know where it was, but it was certainly not here. Not of this earth. My first thought, as soon as the medicine kicked in, was that I was afraid to die. And that felt like a real possibility. I've always thought of myself as someone who is relatively at peace with death. I commune with the other side; I know that even once our body is gone from this current life, our soul lives on. But the feeling that I was experiencing under the influence of the medicine—it was new to me. I didn't feel high. I felt like I'd been transported to a whole other universe, and the idea that I might never come back truly scared me. I like my life, I realized, and I like where I am in my journey with myself. I know little tiny morsels about the other side, but while I'm in this life there's no real way to know what it's like, and I'm not ready to find out yet.

I was wearing the blindfold during the entire ceremony, so while I couldn't see in the literal sense, I could see clearly in my mind's eye. Soon after the medicine kicked in, I was visited by what looked like a kundalini snake. It was tall and coiled and stared at me with its beady eyes. I admitted to the snake that I was scared, and that this was way scarier than I had expected. "I'm right here," she said.

"But I'm going to die," I said. "I can tell."

"You already died," she said. "You asked for this. I didn't come to you, you came to me. You have died over and over again, and you have been born over and over again. There is no life or death."

This interaction with the snake went on for a long while—or what felt like a long while. On this journey, time was not a factor. I found out later that I was on the medicine for nine hours, but you could have told me it was three days. At some point, Kirsty told me I needed to scream. She screamed first, and then I screamed, and it was as if the scream came from my fucking vagina. It was so loud and so deep and so guttural that Kirsty said it shook the windows. I imagined that people from down the mountain could hear it. As for me, not only could I hear the scream but I could *see* it. The vibrations appeared directly in front of me.

At some point, my blindfold slipped down a bit, which made it quite clear to me why I needed that blindfold in the first place. The entire world looked like a cartoon, and that was terrifying. Everything was morphing and shape-shifting, and while my physical being was on the planet, I was in a completely different world. Or worlds, really. Not only did I travel back in time to moments in my life where core wounds were established, I also traveled back into my past lives. Most memorable was a journey back into the life of Bessie, an enslaved woman who worked in the cotton fields. In the moment I caught her, she was taking the cotton, because it was all she had, and she was planting it into the Earth. It was her prayer to God, because she knew the Earth was God, just as I know the same today. "This is the only offering I have," she was saying. "It can't be for nothing."

What I heard Bessie say, or maybe it was me who was saying it, was that God had to make this right—this horror, this hell she lived in, it had to be made better somehow, some way. Even if it wasn't in her lifetime. What I could see clearly during this visit was that slavery was so much more savage than we even know or believe it to have been.

Bessie would eventually get raped by her owner and get pregnant. I know that because I was suddenly transported to that place, sitting on the floor, legs spread, simulating giving birth to a child. I *was* Bessie in a past life, but in this life she wanted to visit and remind me what I'd already been through. That I'd already survived.

Eventually, I moved on from Bessie and into another life. It was a man this time. He might have been enslaved at one point too, I'm not totally sure. But if Bessie was there to remind me of the pain and difficulty I'd already endured, this man was there to show me that I could find peace. He was wild and free—he had released himself from his past and was now experiencing nirvana. I felt his peace for only a fleeting moment, but it was enough to convince me that it is possible. I was one with him, living amid the most beautiful grass and bright sun and stunning sky. I was surrounded by planets and many moons. It wasn't the Earth that I know in this life, but it was a place free from worry. One where everything was perfect. I felt his nirvana, if only for an instant.

My next visit was to the incubator from my infancy. I was in the body of baby Bea, just of out her mother's womb. I felt a mixture of fear and sadness and loneliness. As a baby, I didn't have the opportunity to breastfeed or get skin-to-skin contact. I didn't receive the physical love and comfort a baby deserves, through no fault of mine or my mother's. I was in a tiny body that didn't know how to walk or talk or ask for what it needed, but now I was seeing this situation from the vantage point of an adult, and I could recognize this trauma for what it was. As Baby Bea, I knew that I needed love and attention, but I couldn't communicate those needs to anyone else. I had to rely on other people to know what help I required and provide it. I couldn't do anything alone, not even breathe, and I was deeply frustrated.

Looking out from the eyes of my infant self, it was clear to me that everyone was feeling bad for me. But even then, in my tiniest form, I didn't want pity. My mother's family and friends would come to my incubator and peer at me through the plastic with eyes full of sorrow. They wanted so much to be able to help, but I didn't want their help. I just wanted out. I was comfortable, and I was grateful to be alive and to be tended to by so many caring souls, but I wanted to feel normal. I was tired of the tubes. I was tired of being encased in plastic. I just wanted to be with my mom, with no barriers between us. I wanted all these other humans—beautiful humans who made sure I survived and treated me only with care—to disappear and leave me with the woman who had brought me into this world. The one who believed in me from before she even knew for sure that I was in her womb. I wanted more than anything to escape the plastic box and be with my mother, unencumbered by wires or breathing devices, and so I considered it my responsibility to stay alive.

Although all the help and support I received in the hospital as a baby was necessary, and I probably wouldn't have survived without it, clearly I carried some amount of resentment too for the simple fact that I needed it. During that visit, I realized that because I was so physically weak as a baby, I equated asking for help with admitting weakness. I decided by the time I was only two days old that that would never be me.

This visit to the incubator was accompanied by a visit from my spirit guides, who told me I had to get more comfortable asking for help. Not just praying, which I have always done, but really asking for things and meaning it, in all areas of my life. I began to sob, probably because I was on medicine and I was so wide open that emotions could pour out of me like water through a faucet, but also because their words touched a very deep wound. I do hold back from asking for help, especially from people who are close to me. I don't want to ask too much of them, or seem too vulnerable, so I resist. And yet there is something really beautiful about getting taken care of by people who love you. Especially when you are usually the caretaker and the giver and the healer, all of which I am.

My time on the medicine was a journey through my past lives and my current one, and a plunge into my consciousness. It forced me to confront deep-seated thoughts and traumas that I was clinging to even though they weren't serving me. The serpent who called out my fear of death, and the guides who exposed my resistance to asking for help—they each provoked literal confrontations. The experience forced me to relive moments so that I could observe them as an outsider, see them more objectively, and ultimately release them. It showed me the level of peace that is possible one day, and also highlighted the necessity of staying on my current professional path. In fact, when my guides spoke to me about asking for help, they

And yet there is something really beautiful about getting taken care of by people who love you. Especially when you are usually the caretaker and the giver and the healer, all of which I am.

emphasized that the Honey Pot work is what I was put on the planet for—empowering people with vaginas to love themselves and heal themselves. Because of how important and necessary that work is, they said, if I needed help, I had to seek it. I owed it to the humans I serve. They explained to me that all women have goddess energy and by helping my customers to home in on that, even if it's just by erasing the shame around vaginal wellness, I am doing holy work. There's a lot of masculine energy in this world, they said, which makes it a hard place to be a person with a vagina. If we can open ourselves to healing, we can find liberation, and I needed to help facilitate that, alone or with the aid of others.

Nine hours after I took that dose of mushrooms and began my ceremony, I was back on this planet, and back in this body. I was relieved to be alive, but also completely changed. I felt freer. Lighter. While in ceremony, the medicine and the setting and the sensory deprivation and the people who were there to guide me and keep me safe—all of those factors created an atmosphere that allowed me to let down my guard and tap into myself in ways that wouldn't have been readily available otherwise. Our psyches are powerful agents of protection, so much so that we can have traumatic experiences and almost immediately block them from our memories. Some people consider mushrooms and similar therapies taboo, but I see them as spirit and soul work. I am not a medical doctor or researcher, but I do believe my time on the medicine enabled me to confront traumas I'd been hiding from myself, not because I was in denial but because I was in protection mode. Studies have found that psilocybin can increase connections between brain regions and increase neural growth, helping individuals suffering with afflictions like depression or PTSD or cluster headaches. I won't deny that I was scared out of my mind for some of my time on that journey, but I do believe it opened my eyes to so many truths about myself that I needed to acknowledge, and that it changed my life for the better.

I embarked on the mushroom ceremony because I knew there was a lot of mess from my past that I hadn't dealt with and didn't have the capacity to deal with on my own. My brain simply wouldn't let me. I needed to force myself into a circumstance where all I could do was go inward. That's what these medicine rituals are all about, and what shamans have been doing for hundreds of years—using the Earth's offerings to help humans tap into the source of who we are and where we come from. There was a lot I needed to process and get through and heal from in that ceremony. My ex-husband, sure, but also the fact that I'd been working pretty much my entire life—since I got my first job at fifteen years old—and was worn down and carrying the burden of someone who'd felt she had to fend for herself at such a young age. There are plenty of people who've been working longer than that, I know, but I've lived a full life, and the work I've done hasn't always felt good for my soul.

All of this shit was heavy, and I needed to get it off me. We each have our own layers of muck—wounds we haven't processed for whatever reason. And it's not like you do a mushroom ceremony and suddenly, voilà, you're healed and you will never suffer again. No, you'll still go through trauma and drama and conflict. That will continue forever, because you are a human being in the world. But it's important, from time to time, to acknowledge some of the hardest stuff you've been through and stare those motherfuckers down until you've exterminated them or truly healed from them. I want to live with levity and enjoy myself and not be defined by my trauma. I want to appreciate water and food and clothes and be good to people and appreciate all that makes life beautiful. It's hard to do that when you're still grappling internally with events from your past or people who have hurt you. It's hard to enjoy the present moment when stubborn past moments are sitting on your soul. Even if it's only happening subconciously, which is very often the case. Until we unearth all that gunk, there will always be a piece of us stuck in it, rather than living right here.

But it's important, from time to time, to acknowledge some of the hardest stuff you've been through and stare those motherfuckers down until you've exterminated them or truly healed from them.

And being present is a lifelong pursuit. It's not like you figure out how to do it and then cross a finish line. But for me, sitting in the here and now starts with taking care of my spirit and my soul and all these versions of myself that are living inside me, rooted in the past. I want those versions of Bea to understand that we don't have to be stuck. We can keep moving. We can be happy and successful. And we will be.

A mushroom ceremony is akin to a cleanse for the soul, but it's not a one-and-done situation. Let's say you decide to go on a fast, because you want to give your body a clean slate and rid yourself of toxins. Great. Still, if you immediately return to eating food that doesn't nourish you, you'll find your body right back to where you started. Or maybe you deep clean your house. That's well and good but it will be a wreck again in no time if you don't do regular upkeep once the big overhaul is done.

Since the mushroom ceremony, I have been focused on the upkeep of my soul and my spirit. For me, that means fostering a combination of spirituality and religion. It's a union I've fine-tuned to fit my current life. I try to live in a space where I am tapped into my soul, my body, my spirit, my ancestors, and all that makes me who I am, and I try to live in that space every day. There was a time when I was practicing specific religious rituals daily, and that level of strict observant practice was what I needed. But now that I feel more confident and in control and knowledgeable about my religion, one I've practiced for over a decade, the way I practice is in *knowing* that I am connected, at my core, and then just letting myself flow. I know my saints are always walking with me. I've learned that I have about forty-seven ancestors that walk with me at any given time. Some are blood relatives, others are friends, others are people that I have known in previous lives. Of course, forty-seven is more than most people have, but that number is a product of how much I honor them. I acknowledge them. If that's not a custom you've been taught—and most of us in American culture haven't been taught to respect and honor or call out the names of those that came before us, even though they are the reason we are here on this planet—then you won't nurture those relationships. But because I have done that, they are always present to help me if I need them. Sometimes they will whisper to me or come to me in a dream. They'll say, "We're fine, we don't need anything, take care of yourself." They tell me, "If you want to be good to us, be good to you. If you want to love us, love you." There is a humbleness, I hope, to the way I practice because I don't want to just use my saints, I want to respect and honor them. Sometimes I can sense that it's time to get a reading, or to serve them in another way, and I do that. But I'm tapped into myself and into my saints simultaneously, because I know we are the same thing.

This way of living, I think of it as the religion of me. Everything from my meditation practice to my work with my intuitive to my Reiki healing to my chiropractor to my religious rituals, it all helps me keep myself intact. And as a soul that is in a body on this planet for maybe the hundreth time, I've accepted that this is what is necessary for me to operate. We are all so vulnerable—we are literally beings wrapped in skin, underneath which billions and trillions of interactions are happening at a cellular level in the exact sequence necessary to survive. That's a crazy miracle when you stop to think about it, so I consider it my responsibility to do whatever is necessary to honor that miracle and exist at my fullest capacity.

Spirituality is very personal. Religion too. It's important to me that I'm not practicing just to practice. To me, true spiritual and religious practice is in how you are living every day of your life. How you are treating people and taking care of yourself. That you are not over-giving. All of that, to me, is a manifestation of God. In fact, everything is God. Me, you, the air, the plants, the water that I drink and the food that I eat, and the love that I have for my mother or the love that I have for someone I've just met. I know now that God isn't just one thing. I know that God is everything, everywhere, all the time, all at once. I had to go through a lot of shit—intense hardship and intense healing—to fully understand that, but now that I do, I live with much more reverance. The fact that I can sit in a chair in a house that I bought with my hard-earned money and write a book. Having survived the entirey of my life experiences. I am so grateful for all of it. That is my ministry; that is my spirituality; that is my God.

It would be presumptuous, and simply not accurate, to say I've reached complete peace and enlightenment. I am a work in progress. I still carry traumas; I am still working to shed them. But I've come a long way. I've grown. I've made it. And that's important for me to remember. When things get hard, I ask myself: *Where are you now? Are you well? Do you have water and food and a house? Can you go on a trip? Can you smile?* This is what I go back to: I've made it, I'm here, I'm alive.

Chapter Eleven

Love Yourself, Set Yourself Free

Not long ago, I was in Cuba for another religious trip, and the priest doing my reading asked me what felt like a pointed question. "How do you see yourself?" he said. I didn't know how to answer. For better or worse, I have never spent much time reflecting on my accomplishments or how I do the work that I do. I don't think about how I see myself, I barely take time to see myself at all.

"Uh, I'm a human," I said hesitantly. "I'm a happy person. I'm flowing. I'm busy."

He looked, shall we say, not thrilled with my answer.

"OK, if you were to ask me the same question, here's how I'd answer," he said. "I would say, I am thirty years old, I own two homes, I am successful, I have traveled the world, I have close relationships." He continued on in this manner for a bit. The point was, he would own his accomplishments. He would be proud of them.

I've always worked very hard not to eat the ego food. Leading a company comes with a lot of eyeballs, as I've already mentioned. There is a lot of acknowledgment. A lot of rewards and awards. It mostly comes from a good place, but I got so fixated on not getting a big head and not letting the ego food distract me from my mission that I began to tell myself a story that I had to keep my head down and keep moving and be grateful for the accomplishments but never get caught up in them. That was how I'd stay true to who I am. The narrative I created was *If you relish in your success, you are ungrateful. If you acknowledge it at all, you are prideful. If you stop to admire how far you've come, you have lost your way.*

What that priest was trying to tell me was that you can do both. You can be proud of yourself *and* be grateful. You can look at yourself in the mirror and say, "I am doing a great job. I am successful, kind, beautiful, achieving, and manifesting," *and* still be humble. You can be confident and not let it go to your head. That has been incredibly hard for me. It still is. I'm practicing though. I'm figuring out how to look in the mirror and say, "I'm beautiful, I'm amazing, I'm successful, I'm a winner." And not just how to say it, but how to be OK with saying it. That doesn't come naturally.

When the priest showed me the difference between my

answer, which was really a nonanswer, and his, which was clear and specific and true, I started to cry. I'm tearing up just writing about it, and I'm not entirely sure why. Is there a part of me that's scared that if I acknowledge my success, it will go away? Is there a deep-seated inner Bea who feels undeserving, despite the work that I've put in? I've had moments of low self-esteem when it comes to relationships—am I scared that if I own my success and speak my pride aloud, that I won't be seen as lovable? I still don't really know. The beautiful thing is, I don't have to know. I don't have to have the answers immediately. I have time. But I am paying attention now.

In January of 2024, Honey Pot made a big announcement: We'd partnered with an investment company who bought a majority stake in our business. This was the outcome of the process we began soon after my trip to Mexico. We were at the stage and scale and size financially that it was time to find to new partner. It was also time to give our earlier backers an opportunity to see a return on their investment and for those of us who'd been working at Honey Pot to have a chance to see the fruits of our labor. The process of finding our next partner was everything I'd expected it to be: a combination of excitement, fear, nerves, and extreme exhaustion. There were incredibly late nights and lots of intense stress. We worked with a managing consulting firm to help us build a case for who we are and what we do. I must have been on seventy-five planes during that process, flying to meet with various potential partners. We sat through hours and hours of meetings, created pages and pages of presentations, and let firm after firm dig into our data. I'm grateful for the experience, because I know it's one that most founders only dream of, but it was exhausting. Honestly, it was nearly impossible, which is exactly why most founders don't get to do it.

We met plenty of potential partners who didn't work out, sometimes because they felt it wasn't a fit and other times because we did. Finding the right partnership is not just about money. You also have to consider what happens after you exchange the money. What happens to the business, to the team, and to how we manage the operations? Will this partner trust us to run the company, or do they want to take over everything themselves? One company told me they wanted to move me into the role of "brand ambassador," which quickly told me they didn't want me to stay on as CEO. They thought they could do a better job, which was a clear indication to me that they weren't the right partner. My team and I are the best people to build this business. I know that for a fact. So if a partner didn't want to keep us on, it told me we didn't share a long-term vision.

With the partnership we landed on, I am still the CEO and chief innovation officer. I still hold a substantial minority stake in the company—which is to say, I am still seriously tied to this business and its success. It was not a situation where a major conglomerate came along and bought us out and my team and I cashed out and walked away. What people who see announcements of investments on Instagram but aren't well versed in start-ups often don't understand is that if you get an investment like we did, the investors usually want company leadership to reinvest 25–50 percent of whatever equity they have back into the business. They want to be sure you have skin in the game. If you cash out completely, then you'll be ultra-wealthy and you may not have a need for your company anymore. That matters to them, because in the kind of partnership we forged, it's our expertise and contributions that will lead the business to a place of success. Our partner knew that when they invested in our business, they were also investing in the people who ran it. They didn't want us to bounce. They wanted us to stay and keep the company on the path to success. They wanted our creativity and know-how and intuition. Luckily, that's what I wanted too.

Honey Pot isn't just a financial endeavor for me. Money is fantastic and I'm very grateful for it, but it's only a small part of why I do what I do. It pales in comparison to my commitment to helping people love their bodies and educating humans about their vaginas and being an example of change in the world. That's why I wake up every day. So me and my team are still logging in, working harder than ever to move our company toward our ultimate goal of becoming the largest personal care brand in the world. Still, creating our partnership was a milestone moment. It meant that the members of our team, many of whom had been with us since Honey Pot was a baby, would experience something beautiful and get paid back for their blood, sweat, and tears with something tangible that could go directly into their bank accounts. It also meant the investors who'd been with us and believed in us from the beginning would get their money back fifty or sixty times, which meant the bet they'd made on The Honey Pot Company, and on us, was a smart and successful one. I was able to experience the beginnings of wealth, which is incredibly new to me, while still being tied to this company and having the privilege of continuing to work for its progress. If I had a dollar for every time someone has asked, since learning of this deal, "Are you working less now?" . . . well, I'd probably be able to retire altogether. But no, I still work forty hours and then some; I still travel a few days a week. It's as if I was given some pillows to put under my legs when I lie down at night, but I've still gotta wake up and do the work when the morning comes.

The moment the news of our investment went out, the internet went wild, as it does. I'd made a concerted effort to communicate the announcement carefully, because people are always itching to create a narrative, and the truth can so easily get skewed. I posted a statement that I hoped made clear we'd forged a partnership, not made a sale. But the internet is savage, and the story got twisted a bit, with plenty of people assuming, and even reporting, that I was stepping down or that we'd had a total buyout. There would have been nothing wrong with that if it had been the case, but it wasn't, and for a moment I let that spread of misinformation get me down. I have given so much love and care to this company that it's still hard for me when anonymous online lurkers twist information to fit their agenda, or when a misunderstanding fosters more misunderstanding. The reality was that we did what businesses do—we raised money and made a strategic partnership. That's standard operating procedure. But I only let this misperception affect me for a little while. I'd learned from our past, and I'd grown. That is all we can ever ask for.

While it wasn't a total buyout, I won't deny that the money that came from this deal has put me a step closer to living the life of abundance that I have long envisioned for myself. I am a person who likes nice things and wants to live well. I like having nice clothes, I like traveling, I like getting an Uber Black. I enjoy flying first class or buying a cute dress or hoodie when I see it. I like the fact that my mom is taken care of and her bills are paid and she doesn't have to worry. I am not going to apologize for that because I earned all of it, and I did so honorably.

But the success I've seen thus far is meaningful for reasons far bigger than money. It is proof of what's possible for me, and what is possible in the world. Being able to cash a check based on my work at Honey Pot tells me that it's possible to do good in the world and still make a profit. It's possible to sell beautiful, efficacious products that are tested at a mass scale and still not sell your soul. It's possible to inspire people through products and conversation. It's possible to sow your love and passion for helping others into your business. It's possible to be a human of color who raises a ton of money and sells some of her equity so she can see wealth. It's possible to have a dream and work hard and actually see something come of it. And even when the ultimate goal is still just a glimmer in the distance, it's possible to have milestone moments along the way.

To be clear, I'm still striving. I want to get to a place where I don't have to think about how my house is being cleaned, how my clothes are going to get to the dry cleaner's, how my food will get on my table. My house is my church, my everything. It's where I lay my head at night, which is one of the most vulnerable and spiritual things you can do, and I want that space to be taken care of. I dream of a life where I have a family—a partner and children—that I can enjoy in houses around the world, in cities where there is a jungle and an ocean and clean air. I want to live in a major metropolitan area, and a couple of times a year I want to go and spend a month or two in Europe. I want to eat good food and enjoy the art on my walls. All of that takes means. Not to mention the fact that I want a life where I have an abundance of help with my kids and my home and my lifestyle, not from servants, but from people who I respect and who I in turn treat well, which absolutely includes paying them well. I don't want money so that I can roll around in piles of cash. I want it because I know it's necessary to create this beautiful existence I dream of, and to distribute wealth in turn.

And even when the ultimate goal is still just a glimmer in the distance, it's possible to have milestone moments along the way.

Right now, I am designing and organizing my life in order to get to the place I just described. It takes focus and precision. All the pieces of my current existence are deliberately set up to serve this goal. My time and my energy and my manifestation and my vitamins and the plants in my house and the water that I drink—all of this needs to be in order to make my life flow in the direction I want it to. But I am working every day for that abundance because I do not feel entitled to any of it. I know what it will take to make it all happen and I want to earn it.

As far as I have come professionally, the biggest evidence of my mental, emotional, and spiritual evolution these days comes not in the form of my work but in the state of my relationships. I've always found the professional side of my life to be a bit easier than the personal one. Not easier in the sense that it took less work—I've been slogging through mud since I was a teenager, trying to do the work to provide for myself—but professionally, the equation felt more clear. If I hustled my ass off and added some smarts and some passion and a little bit of luck, it would equal success eventually. I fully believed that, even if I had absolutely no sense of when that equal sign would appear. I've always felt deserving of professional success. I believed I was earning it, and knew that when I did I would be entitled to it. But when it comes to relationships, I have much more fear and insecurity. I don't know that I've always felt deserving of rich and nourishing relationships. After my

But I am working every day for that abundance because I do not feel entitled to any of it. I know what it will take to make it all happen and I want to earn it.

marriage, I harbored a lot of disappointment in myself for staying as long as I did. I was angry that I'd allowed myself to be in a situation where I was treated with less care than I deserved. That wasn't the kind of person I wanted to be, and it was hard to live with myself for a while. I knew I would never consider myself entitled to a good relationship until I could begin to forgive myself for being in a bad one.

After I got divorced, I had a couple of short-lived romances. Each had its own perks—the dick was good; a friendship was forming—but they were each a little off balance, probably because I still didn't know what I wanted from a relationship. Also, with each one I got better at recognizing my own unhealthy patterns, and spotting the moment when I began to repeat them. I was paying enough attention to find myself at the beginnings of an awakening. I've said that at Honey Pot I am a proponent of failing fast, but over time the same has become true of romance. I don't want to just wait and see anymore, hoping that any obstacles to compatability or happiness will fall away over time. If I see myself slipping into bad patterns, I want to cut it off and move on. So in those short-lived romances, that's what I did. They didn't last long enough for me to even think about a future.

Recently, my soul instinct has led me to realize that the relationship I really need to focus on—before I can find genuine satisfaction in any romance—is my relationship with myself. Yes, I've been practicing self-care through bodywork, spirituality, exercise, and hydration. But now, I don't just want to care for myself—I want to know myself. That is the next frontier.

When people ask me, "What do you need?" I want to know the answer. What do I need from my friends? From my family? From my guides and ancestors? From my lovers? From myself?

When I look back on my life, I see how much time I've spent working, planning, building, and being everything to everyone—often at the expense of sitting still with Bea. It's wild to me that I've found it easier to create a business plan, name it, trademark it, and bring it to life than to simply sit with the person I've been my entire life and truly get to know her. What are her inner desires? What makes her feel valued? What brings her peace? What makes her sing?

Lately, I've been discovering the sacred power of stillness. When you really sit with yourself—without distraction, without agenda—you begin to see yourself clearly. You begin to feel what you've been avoiding. You hear the whispers beneath the noise. Sitting with yourself is an act of devotion. It's not about isolation; it's about intimacy. It's where you meet your truth without interruption.

Sitting with yourself is an act of devotion.

Stillness reveals what you truly need. It shows you what feels aligned and what does not. It gives you clarity where confusion used to live. And the deeper I go into that silence, the more I realize that love—real, sustaining love—begins there.

So right now, instead of searching for love elsewhere, I am searching for it here, inside myself, inside Beatrice Nikka Dixon. That starts by investigating what love even means. What does it mean to love yourself? Or even to like yourself?

Love involves friendship, kindness, grace, and appreciation. I want to be a friend to Bea. To show her kindness and grace. To appreciate her.

It's a hard concept to wrap my head around, and I think that's true for many women. We hold up the world around us. We wake up thinking, *What do I have to do today? Who do I have to serve? What does my partner need? What do my kids need*? We are nurturers by nature, which means we must go the extra mile to care for ourselves. I want to wake up and take the first five minutes just for me. I don't yet know what that would feel like in my body or in my soul—but I want to.

Knowing myself and learning what I need requires brutal honesty. Because what you need is not always what you want. I may want the big sweeping romance—and maybe I'll have it one day—but only after I truly understand what I need and how to ask for it.

Of course, the relationship that has been the most constant in my life is the one with my mother. She is my warrior. My best friend. My mirror. She often knows what's happening with me before I do. She has been my anchor in every season of my becoming, and for that, I am endlessly grateful.

I'm not ruling out the possibility of romantic love. But I no longer subscribe to society's definition of what success in love should look like. I don't need a certificate, a title, or a grand performance to validate my capacity to love or be loved. I need authenticity. I need peace. I need alignment.

All we can do is keep learning.

And the more I learn, the clearer it becomes that the journey back to self is the greatest love story there is.

So if you're reading this—pray for me as I continue to learn how to sit with myself. And know that I am praying for you, too. May you slow down enough to meet the truth of who you are. May you find comfort in your own company. May you discover the still, sacred power that lives within you.

Because when we sit with ourselves long enough, we find that everything we've ever been searching for . . . has been sitting quietly inside us all along.

On paper, I know my life seems right where I should want it to be. It's probably easy to look at it from the outside, to read these pages, and think, *She's finally made it. So much has changed. A storybook ending!* And if I ever had the time, or the inclination, to sit back and take stock of my life, I might even feel that way too. When I look at where I am today, it does feel different, *and* it feels like one foot in front of the other. It feels like things have changed *and* like they've stayed exactly the same, because work still has to be done across all areas of my life. Both are true. I move through the world differently—with more comfort and stability and safety—but I still bust my ass to get products off the ground and innovate for the future. I feel more settled in my healthy relationship, *and* I continue to work on myself to be a better friend, family member, and colleague.

When I take stock of my life at the present moment, at

least from certain angles, it looks crazier than ever. Despite my renewed focus on stillness, life is more hectic than it's ever been. I'm busy, but it's a different kind of busy. It's as if all the moments that came before—they were busy school. It was about getting by and learning what I needed to survive in the short term, but it also equipped me for the long game. All those challenges I had to overcome, they were preparing me for this moment. Sure, I was working multiple jobs and feeling stressed and trying to figure my shit out, but I didn't have as much on my back as I do now. I had to take care of myself, and sometimes my mom, but I didn't serve a collective greater good. I wasn't working for a bigger population than our little twosome. But now I think of those days as busy school. Hustle school. Earn school.

Today, when I look back at any of the hardships I've been through in my life—whether it was dancing on a pole or fucking a couple for money or not having a place to call home or just barely making the bread to pay rent—I see them as preparation. I believe my life path was paved for greatness, but heavy is the head that wears the crown. Usually, the people who wear the crowns have been through some shit, because you have to be ready for what the crown is going to bring. You have to be able to handle its weight, and that comes with experience. The busy I feel today, sure it's overwhelming occasionally, but it feels purposeful. It doesn't feel dysfunctional or unhealthy. This busy is bigger than me, but I can handle it. When I was younger and going through shit and living and flowing and trying to figure out how to get from here to there, that busy was just for me. But this busy is not just for Beatrice. It is for the humans I serve and for the people I love. It is for creating small bits of change in the world. It is for wanting to be good to the people I work with and the people I make products for. This busy has depth and it's beautiful and hard and carries a lot of responsibility. It can be heavy but it can also be light and fun. Sometimes it's proud and sometimes it's meek. It has a lot of layers to it, and the stakes feel higher than ever. But I am ready, because I am prepared.

When I really dial into my deepest desire right now, my truest goal for my being, it is that I take care of myself. Self-care has gotten a bad rap these days. It was popular, but then it became a parody of itself, a trope of face masks and bubble baths as actual problem-solvers. In common vernacular, it seems to have lost all meaning. But I take it seriously. Honey Pot is what I do. It is my life's work, but it is my *work*. For so long, all I did was work. It was all I thought about. I ate, breathed, shit, pissed, fucked work. But there is only so much time that you can spend working at that pace. Today, more than a decade after starting this business, I have a whole entire life. It needs to be more than all work all the time, but taking care of myself can be difficult for me. I'll be at home and I'll get into a flow with my workouts and nutrition and my water and then I'll get on the road and be like, *fuck, I'm tired.* Part of me wants to go for a walk but part of me is like, *Bea, you should lay down.* I'll want to eat healthy, but then I eat the gluten in that muffin because, frankly, it looks delicious. Or

I know I shouldn't eat beef because I have an intolerance to it, but there is a place in New York that only makes, like, sixteen burgers a night. On one hand, knowing what it can do to my body, eating it is probably not self-care. But maybe I *am* taking care of myself, because I am feeding my body and soul something they crave. I want to live well and enjoy myself. I want to ensure that throughout all of this work and business travel and growth, I don't get so focused on outcomes that I forget about Bea. The question I am asking myself, nearly every day, is *Do you like how your life is? And if you don't, are you willing to do the work to change what feels lacking?*

I am willing to do the work. To keep doing the work. Because I like how my life is, but for all its abundance, there is also lack. There are aspects of myself I want to change. As much as I know that there's an ancient part of me that comes from another planet and has lived many lives, as much as I know that my soul has survived centuries and will live on after this body does not, I still exist right now in this human incarnation. I'm still living on this planet and having this human experience just like everybody else. And with that comes very human emotions. I have stuff I want to work on just like everyone else. Luckily, learning to acknowledge my accomplishments without eating the ego food has gotten me closer to acknowledging my shortcomings without feeling angry at myself or wallowing in self-blame. I can observe my life—my strengths and weaknesses, my haves and have-nots—without attaching too much emotion.

To that end, the list of things I want to work on starts with quieting my inner critic. Even though there's a large part of me that doesn't believe in the constructs that society has built around race and gender, I am also a product of those constructs, which means I sometimes have insecurities about being a Black human, or a Black woman in business. I can observe the double standards, the extra obstacles that are put in my path, and still question myself when I don't find success as easily as someone else. I want to quiet that voice until I can't even remember what it sounds like.

But we all have an ego. I can work forever toward letting mine go, but I will never be free of it altogether. Nobody can kill the ego entirely. That's OK. After all, it serves a purpose. It's there to protect us and remind us who we are. But when it affects our relationships and lifestyle and self-love, then it's important to understand when we need to die to it and release it as much as possible. My work, when it comes to my ego and insecurities, needs to be focused on seeing those moments for what they are and saying to myself *that's something I need to work on*, without making a value judgment. The only way I can change is to actively think about how to change. To look for the source of my ego or shame or hurt and to go back to that version of Bea, the one who first developed that insecurity, and talk to her. I need focus on mending *that* little girl, or that young woman, or that full-blown adult. That's where the magic starts. That's how habits and behavior and self-talk begin to change.

But I want to remember that I am not bad for feeling insecure, and I am not good for feeling secure. I just am.

When I think about what it means to live an abundant life, I think of contentedness and wellness and the ability to take a shower and go to sleep at night. It's the bare minimum of existence that most of us take for granted, although not everyone has even that. That doesn't mean you don't hustle and bust your ass to make your bread, but that you do it while keeping in mind that what matters more than a fat check is knowing how not to be an asshole. And knowing that you are not better than anyone else. And knowing how to hold a conversation—with a woman who dances on a pole just as easily as one who is a CEO. If I could impart one lesson that I know from experience, it's that we are all just trying to make it through the day and face the world with as much bravery as we can muster.

The goal of the work I'm doing in these pages is not to be able to say, *Ta-da! Happy ending!* It's to be able to answer the question my priest asked me, and a few more at that: *How do I see myself? Where am I now? How did I get here? What am I working toward?*

Writing a book certainly makes you consider these questions. Any meaningful soul work does. So, how do I see myself? I've thought about how I might answer the priest's question today. Here's a second try: I am a founder. I am a seeker. I am driven. I am a giver. Sometimes I can be a slave to that, to the giving, to the point where it leads to resentment. But it's who I am and I don't know how to be anything else. I am naturally going to give all that I have to everything I do, whether that's my work or my life or my family or my lover or my partner. I will give everything my full self because if I put my time and energy into something, I don't know any other way to do it. I am learning to speak up for myself, which is easier for me in some areas than others. It's especially hard for me in matters of the heart, because I've been burned in the past, and because I'm not always living in my feminine energy. The nature of my life and the role I play in my company often requires me to pull from the masculine part of me. The performer and the worker bee. I am in the best relationship I've ever been in, and I'm learning a lot about myself by loving someone else. I am designing my life and doing it well, from the way I keep my home to the fragrances I surround myself with to the way I like to travel. I know how to earn and I live an abundant life, but sometimes that abundance can feel like a lot.

Everything I just said is true. I am all of those things, and yet still I am working toward more. I am evolving. I am working at giving myself an opportunity for real freedom. Not financial freedom but freedom of the mind. Because when you are free in your mind, you are fucking *free*. I've worked really hard at being free financially, in part because I thought it would lead to freedom of the soul. It helps, but only the tiniest bit. Until recently, I would have said I'd already worked at being free in my mind, and maybe I've dabbled, but I realize now that I haven't had the bandwith to fully dig in yet. I've done one-offs, like the mushroom ceremony, but consistent and deliberate work has eluded me. So that's the next step. To not hold the things I don't have to hold. To release hardships I was born with in my DNA structure because of what my family and ancestors went through. To release traumas. To communicate with the parts of myself that sit inside me, still stuck despite my best efforts, and say *We are over forty now. We are successful. We are not our past, or our worst experiences.* But anything that has been sitting for ten, twenty, thirty years—that shit is going to take time to sort out and handle and mend. I am trying to do the work on those parts to heal them and give them the energy they deserve. Because I have to take care of myself. Achieving a certain level of professional and financial success is satisfying, but it's also telling. I've been able to put some money in my pocket, but you get the bread and then what? You are still you. If you can't find peace in your mind and body and soul, you are poor. Proper peace, I believe now, is when you are cool and relaxed and you don't take on other people's problems automatically, though you can if you choose to. It's when you are giving yourself grace. When you know you are a work in progress and you can still have fun and enjoy yourself. All that is what I'm striving for.

I hope there is much more to my story. I have been Bea the preemie, Bea the pharmacist tech, Bea the dancer, Bea the cleaner, Bea the model, Bea the wife, Bea the food broker, and Bea the CEO. I know I will discover other versions of myself. The Bea who is a mother. The Bea who spends days doing nothing but lying on the couch and watching TV or reading a book or simply closing her eyes. The Bea who travels the world. Those future versions will come with their own perks and challenges, some that I can anticipate and many more that I cannot. But all things in order. I can't rush those versions of myself. All I can do is serve the Bea who exists right now, and know that my evolution will unfurl before me. I'm a survivor. That was established the day I was born, and it defined the earliest decades of my life. But today I'm doing much more than surviving. I'm living. I'm doing my best.

Acknowledgments

To my mother—thank you for being my mother. For your contribution to my life and my soul. For being my constant teacher, my mirror, and my first soulmate. I love you endlessly.

To my grandmothers, Margaret and Margaret, thank you for your love and constant support. I am nothing without you.

To my heavenly mothers, Oshun and Yemaya—you love me real and deep, and you keep me on my feet. Thank you for guiding me, for helping me hold my head high, and for all that you've done to help me accomplish in this lifetime. Thank you for my soul.

To my fathers, Abraham and Oggun, thank you for fighting for me into eternity. Your love keeps me grounded and secure. I am forever grateful for you.

To Gwyneth—my chosen older sister—thank you for your constant love and friendship, for the way you pour into me and my soul. Thank you truly for supporting me as I tell my story to the world.

To my sisters (you know who you are)—thank you for loving me true, for standing by me, and for helping me become the woman I am.

To the men in my life—our relationships may not have all ended well, but I am grateful for the lessons, for the love, and for our time together.

To my brothers—thank you for your love, your protection, and your support.

To Simon—for your love, friendship, devotion, and belief in me. No matter what happens, you are my chosen brother.

To Rachel Bertsche—thank you for tapping into my mind, heart, and soul. For seeing me. For understanding me. We've been through so much together to get to this point, and I am forever grateful.

To my publishing team—my editor, Lauren Spiegel, thank you for believing in this book and for your brilliant editing. Heather Waters, Kimberly Laws, Jessica Roth, and the entire wonderful team at Gallery Books, your support means the world. I'm deeply grateful for your dedication, excellence, and heart. A special thank you to Johanna Castillo, my beloved agent, and Victoria Mallorga at Writers House for your constant care and guidance.

To my Honey Pot team, and especially to Shameika Chan—I love you all. I deeply appreciate your contributions, your sacrifices, your time, and your devotion. You make beautiful things happen every day. This journey hasn't been easy, but we've done it together.

To every human who chooses to read this story—thank you for believing in me. I pray that this book assists you in your life as much as it has assisted me.

To all the humans who have supported The Honey Pot—you've supported my dream and my life's work. I love you and I am deeply grateful for you.

Lastly, to myself—for always being able to flow, to trust God, my Orishas, my ancestors, and my guides. It hasn't always been easy, but I love you, Bea.

I hope you enjoyed these pages.

The Soul Instinct was written as a self-help book to myself. It was deeply cathartic—even though I told y'all all my business. Please work hard not to judge me for what you've read. I am just a soul trying to navigate life, just like everyone else.

About the Author

Beatrice Dixon is the cofounder, CEO, and chief innovation officer of The Honey Pot Company—the first complete personal wellness brand "made by humans with vaginas, for humans with vaginas®." She has been named one of Goldman Sachs's 100 Most Intriguing Entrepreneurs, *Worth*'s Worthy 100, *Forbes*'s Top 100 Female Founders, *Inc.*'s Top 100 Women Entrepreneurs, Ebony Power 100, and *Create & Cultivate*'s 100.